2007 Edition

Free Stuff for Baby!

How to Save Hundreds of Dollars Every Year on the Things You Need Most

Sue M. Hannah

McGraw·Hill

New York   Chicago   San Francisco   Lisbon   London   Madrid   Mexico City
Milan   New Delhi   San Juan   Seoul   Singapore   Sydney   Toronto

Library of Congress Cataloging-in-Publication Data

Hannah, Sue M.
    Free stuff for baby! : how to save hundreds of dollars every year on the things
you need most / Sue M. Hannah.— 2006–2007 ed.
        p.   cm.
    New ed. of, Free stuff for baby!, 2003.
    ISBN 0-07-145753-4 (book : alk. paper)
      1. Infants' supplies industry—Directories.   2. Free material—Directories.
  I. Title.

  HD9970.5.I542H36   2005
  649'.122'0297—dc22   2005007294

1 2 3 4 5 6 7 8 9 0   DOC/DOC 0 9 8 7 6 5

ISBN 0-07-145753-4

Interior design by Amy Yu Ng

McGraw-Hill books are available at special quantity discounts to use as premiums and sales promotions, or for use in corporate training programs. For more information, please write to the Director of Special Sales, Professional Publishing, McGraw-Hill, Two Penn Plaza, New York, NY 10121-2298, or contact your local bookstore.

This book is printed on acid-free paper.

To Kayla, Shane, and Katie

You have opened up my world with your imagination.

You fill my heart with love. You are my blessings!

Contents

Acknowledgments

Writing this book has been a wonderful experience but definitely a challenge at times. I couldn't have done it without the support and encouragement from many wonderful people, whose names I would like to mention at this time.

A very special thanks to my editors, Michele Pezutti and Julia Anderson Bauer at McGraw-Hill. Thanks for believing in me and giving me this wonderful opportunity!

Many thanks to Catherine McDiarmid and all who contributed their wonderful frugal baby tips at the Born to Love website.

To my mom and dad: It's so comforting to know that you are always there for me, and support me in everything that I do. Through you I have learned to appreciate the simple things in life, the things that are truly important, like spending quality time together and just being there for each other through the good and the bad. Thanks for being present for me every step of the way!

No thanks would be complete without mentioning my ever-faithful support team of friends, family, and relatives:

Don, Cameron, and Amanda Herzberg; Pete, Rebecca, Ashley, and Julia Herzberg; and Paul, Kelly, Alexandria, and Samantha Moffat.

To the doting grandparents, Joan and Al MacDonald, who have
spoiled my kids rotten!
Diane Jacques and family
Janine Green and family

Thank you so much for your help and support at a time when I really
needed it. You're the best!

To my husband: Thanks for playing Super Dad to our three children
while I locked myself away in the basement working on this book. (I am
truly sorry for the time I missed with all of you.) Thanks for believing
in me. I never could have done it without you!

To Kayla, Shane, and Katie: I often hear parents talk about their
child's first step or their child's first words. Yet, as truly precious as those
things are, it is the little things that have melted my heart time and time
again, the little day-to-day experiences that take me away from whatever
I am doing at the time—the way your faces light up when I walk into
the room, the way you run to me in a crowd of strangers, the way you
are consoled by my kisses, or, even more delicious, the first time you
gave me a big kiss and a hug and said, "I love you, Mommy." Those are
the sweet memories that will remain in my heart forever.

Love you all! God bless.

Introduction

One of the few times that you will find companies eager to hand you free things is when you're having a baby. Many new or expecting parents do not know how easy it is to get a free sample or discount on their favorite items. Did you know that many well-known companies give free samples, coupons, and other terrific promotional items for many child care items? It's true! These products are free for the asking. All you have to do is call them (many have toll-free numbers), apply online at their websites, or write to them simply asking them to send you these valuable items.

Yes, You Can Get Something for Nothing!

First of all, if you are a new or expecting parent, congratulations and best wishes! This is a very special time for you, a time you will always cherish.

When I first found out that I was pregnant with my now 4½-year-old twins, Shane and Katie, I felt really excited and blessed to be having two babies and could hardly wait for their arrival. Also at the time being the mother of a 2½-year-old, Kayla, I realized from experience that there could be a significant financial strain when a new child enters the family.

So as the expectant mother of twins, I was desperate to get some financial help for my family, especially after being taken aback by a recent article I had read in a parenting magazine. This article plainly stated the staggering costs involved in raising a child. I was astonished to learn that the average parent will probably spend more than $1,500 on premium disposable diapers by the time a child is potty-trained. With twins on the way, I did some quick calculations in my head, multiplying those figures by two, took a deep breath, and realized that, yes, we really did need some extra help.

After carefully going over the family budget with my husband and deciding on some general cutbacks (e.g., pay-TV, the TV guide, subscriptions to those glossy women's magazines that I just loved to read, book club memberships, and just about everything else we could think of), we still came up short.

I subsequently sat down and tried to think of ways to get a little more help for my family. I spent several hours surfing the Internet, reading through parenting magazines and parenting guides, visiting local department stores, as well as making several calls to different companies that offered baby products to find out what kind of help was out there for new or expecting parents.

Many hours and several phone calls later, I was truly surprised to find that so many companies offered free products or samples to new or expecting parents who contacted them by simply making a toll-free phone call, writing a letter, or applying online—and with no obligation to buy anything! These companies were eager to respond to my requests for free samples and promotional products, and in a couple of weeks my mailbox was flooded with valuable free stuff. I could hardly wait to see what my mailman brought me in the mail each day. I received free gift packs, parenting starter kits, coupons, parenting books and magazines, and tons of samples in the mail. I got samples of almost every brand of diaper and formula on the market, plus I received many free gift items for my babies, including baby bibs, bottles, rattles, and much, much more. (One year later I was still receiving free promotional items in the mail!)

Thanks to these truly generous companies, I have had the luxury of freely sampling brand-name products without having to spend my hard-earned money testing out product after product, trying to find the best ones for my babies. I feel much more prepared and can make informed choices on the types of products that my babies will use—and I have truly loved spoiling my babies with all of these great products.

This book will introduce you to numerous companies that offer free samples and other great products for you or your baby. These free offers not only will save you a lot of money but will give you the opportunity to compare different brands of baby products and choose only the best ones for your baby.

The extensive list of free parenting books, magazines, and other literature is available to educate you on every topic of parenting. The support groups are there for you, simply by calling a toll-free number, when you have a parenting question or concern, or even if you just need someone to talk to. In Chapter 11, "Ways to Stretch Your Dollar," you will learn of practical and simple ways to save even more money. Be sure to check out "My Top-Ten List of Totally Useless Baby Items" in Chapter 12 for some infant unnecessaries, things you can definitely do without.

Chapter 7, "Free Government Resources for New or Expecting Parents," is an extremely valuable section, one that all parents should be made aware of. It will direct you to government programs that offer free financial assistance to low- and middle-income families, programs that provide free nutritious foods to needy families, a listing of available tax credits for new or expecting parents, information on how you can receive free health insurance and medical assistance, free government publications, and various other government assistance programs. This section also outlines maternity and parental benefits and what your rights and entitlements are as a new or expecting parent.

While you're spoiling your new baby with all sorts of fabulous freebies, don't forget to baby yourself—because you deserve a break! Check out Chapter 10, "Mom's Free Stuff," where you can find out where to get some luxurious freebies, just for you, such as free perfume samples, cosmetic and hair care samples, and more. Join as many mailing lists as you can and take advantage of what various companies have to offer.

The freebies in this book really help and can go a long way, but there are other things you can give to your new baby as well: lots of love, hugs, kisses, and cuddles. These are truly the most important things that you can offer your baby—and they're free, too!

Enjoy your free stuff!

Remember

Babies are little for such a short period of time, and for that very short period of time, you, as parents, are the center of their universe, the most important people in the world to them—you rock their world!

It gives me such great pleasure and pride to be a mom to my three beautiful children, Kayla, Shane, and Katie. I am so very grateful to be that special person in their lives.

Enjoy your baby. Cherish every moment!

How the Book Works

The lists that I have compiled for you consist of companies that offer free samples and other great products to residents of the United States and Canada.

About 95 percent of the offers listed in this book are absolutely free, with no strings attached. However, a few listings, while free, require you to pay a small shipping and handling fee and/or send a self-addressed, stamped envelope, which the company can use to mail the product back to you. (The cost of the stamp is well worth it!)

When calling or writing to any of these companies, ask to be placed on their mailing lists for any promotional items, special benefits, or coupons and samples for new or expecting parents. Be prepared to state the due date of your baby. You can register with most of these companies right away, but with some of the companies you may have to wait until your baby is born to register. Some of the companies listed will offer free products and samples only until your baby reaches six months of age, so be sure to register as early as you can. Some companies may require a copy of the infant's birth certificate or newspaper announcement. Be sure to send a photocopy only, not the original.

Unless advised otherwise, address all inquiries "Attn: Customer Service," and be sure to *print* your complete contact information (including your name, street and/or e-mail address, and phone number) in any request that you make to these companies. It might also be a good idea to state the sex of your baby.

Many of the companies listed throughout this book have a multiple-birth program; they will send two, three, or four times the coupons and free samples for parents who are expecting twins, triplets, quadruplets, or more. Be sure to state that you are expecting multiples in your telephone conversation or letter to each company you contact.

Once you've received your freebies in the mail, you may wish to take the time to drop a quick thank-you note in the mail to all responding companies to show your appreciation.

Online Updates for Your Added Convenience

In my quest to keep this book as up-to-date as possible, I have created a website (www.freestuff4baby.com) where readers can go to find postings on the latest and most current company offers. Included on this website will be postings of new offers that have been made available since I wrote this book and offers that have been discontinued, as well as general changes in company information, including address changes and other pertinent changes in contact information. Please feel free to visit my website and browse around.

Have you found any offers in the book or on the website that have been discontinued or changed? Have any of the companies listed in this book changed their toll-free numbers or addresses? Has your request been returned to you for any reason? Please drop me an e-mail (sue@freestuff4baby.com) to let me know—and to tell me what you think of the book. Feel free to send any comments or suggestions you might have. I would love to hear from you. Thanks!

Disclaimer

Despite my best effort to make the information in this book as timely and accurate as possible, some listings will be outdated by the time it reaches your hands. Companies may change their promotional offers from time to time, and you may not always receive the freebies that are listed in this book. Companies may move and change their mailing information and phone numbers. Supplies of some items may be limited.

The companies listed in this book have the right to discontinue or substitute their offers at any time they wish. Their offers are subject to change without notice. If the item or publication you are inquiring about is no longer available, ask if the company has anything new or if the item will be offered at a later time. Be sure to check back again, as companies will often bring an offer back at a later time—or may offer an even newer and better free promotional item!

Please be advised that the publisher cannot be held responsible if you do not receive any particular free item listed in this book or if you receive an item that is different from what has been listed in the book. Do not contact the publisher of this book about unfilled or improperly filled orders.

We have not received payment from any of the companies so they could be listed in this book or could receive a better placement in this book. All companies have been treated equally and are simply listed in alphabetical order for your convenience.

Baby Freebies Delivered
to Your Door

This chapter contains tons of company names and toll-free numbers that parents can write or call to receive free stuff for their baby, including free diapers, baby wipes, formula, bibs and rattles, gift packs and parenting starter kits, gift certificates and coupons, baby food samples, additional freebies for parents of multiples, and much, much more! Join as many mailing lists as you can. Be sure to join early in your pregnancy, or when your baby first arrives, to be sure to get the most benefit from these companies.

American Baby
www.americanbaby.com (click on "Free Offers")

American Baby offers a free gift basket to all new or expectant moms! These gift baskets contain various baby freebies, samples, coupons, and more and are available through your hospital or childbirth educator. If you don't receive your free basket at the hospital where you will be giving birth to your baby, be sure to ask your nurse or other hospital staff about the free *American Baby* Basket for new or expectant mothers. This offer is available to residents of the United States and at participating hospitals only.

Visit the website's "Free Offers and More!" area to receive free products and services for your baby, as well as special savings on products you use every day. Also use it to enter contests and sweepstakes where you can win everything from a year's worth of formula to an entire wardrobe for your baby. *American Baby* also offers an assortment of free e-newsletters, such as "Baby Basics," "Preparing for Pregnancy," and "Free Stuff." Visit the website for details.

❦ Associated Hygienic Products (Drypers)

P.O. Box 8830
Vancouver, WA 98666-8830
In the United States or Canada, call 888-639-5863
www.ahp-dsg.com

Write Drypers and send a copy of your baby's birth certificate or birth announcement, plus return mailing information, to receive free Drypers diaper packages and coupons. Call for further details.

This company has a multiple-birth program for parents of twins, triplets, quadruplets, or more. Drypers will send you one coupon for a free package of Drypers diapers for each child, as well as discount coupons. Parents of multiples can write to the attention of the Drypers multiple-birth program, sending copies of their babies' birth certificates or birth announcement, plus return mailing information.

These offers are available to residents of the United States and Canada.

❦ BabyADE

In the United States, call 800-645-9833 (ext. 2003) (Customer Service)
www.BabyADE.com (click on "Free Sample")

Call, or sign up online to receive a free sample of BabyADE diaper rash cream and a free copy of *Parents Guide to Baby Skin Care*. This offer is available to residents of the United States only.

❧ Baby Orajel
See Del Laboratories.

❧ Beech-Nut Nutrition Corporation
Attn: Promotions
100 South Fourth Street
Suite 1010
St. Louis, MO 63102
In the United States or Canada, call 800-233-2468
www.beech-nut.com (click on "Coupons and Special Offers")

Call or write to receive a free New Parents Pack, with coupons for baby food and baby cereal. The Beech-Nut website also offers discount coupons that you can print out for further savings. See the website for details. This offer is available to residents of the United States.

Call to obtain information on Beech-Nut's label-saving program where you can collect and send in proof-of-purchase labels to receive coupons for baby food. The label-saving program is available to residents of the United States only.

Residents of Canada can call to receive a free thirty-two-page nutrition information booklet with feeding guidelines from Beech-Nut.

This company has a multiple-birth program for parents of twins, triplets, quadruplets, or more. Ask for details.

❧ *Best Wishes* (Canada's Baby Magazine)
Family Communications
65 The East Mall
Toronto, ON M8Z 5W3
In Canada, call 416-537-2604 (sorry, not a toll-free number)

The *Best Wishes* package is presented to new mothers after they give birth. The package includes *Best Wishes*, Canada's baby magazine, together with a great assortment of free samples and coupons. You should receive your package at the hospital or through other health care personnel after you give birth to your baby. Ask at the hospital where you will be giving birth about the free *Best Wishes* package for new or expecting mothers. This offer is available to residents of Canada and at participating hospitals only.

❧ Bottoms Barrier Crème

In the United States, call 877-741-1128
www.bottomsbarrier.com (click on "Free Samples")

Bottoms Barrier Crème is a diaper rash cream made of all natural and organic ingredients. Sign up online or call for a free sample. This offer is available to residents of the United States only.

❧ Canadian Baby Photographers

In Canada, call 800-465-9383
www.canadianbaby.com/new/freegift.htm

Call, or visit the Canadian Baby Photographers website to request a free gift portrait for new parents. This offer is available to residents of Canada only.

❧ Carter's

The William Carter Company
Attn: Multiple Birth Program
224 North Hill Street
Griffin, GA 30223
In the United States or Canada, call 800-241-5066
www.carters.com

Carter's has a multiple-birth program for parents of triplets only. Please send copies of your babies' birth certificates to Carter's to receive free Carter's clothing for your babies. Be sure to state the sex of your babies in your written request. This offer is available to residents of the United States and Canada.

❦ Catalina Lighting

Attn: Consumer Service Department
18191 Northwest 68 Avenue
Miami, FL 33015
In the United States or Canada, call 800-966-7074
www.catalinalighting.com

To receive a free halogen bulb cover safety kit to protect your child from burns, mail a request to Catalina Lighting. In your request, indicate how many kits you require, together with your mailing information. You should allow four to six weeks for delivery. This offer is available to residents of the United States and Canada.

❦ Child Safety Seat Program

See State of Virginia.

❦ Customcraft

In the United States, call 888-533-BABY
www.shopbirthannouncements.com (click on "Request a
   Catalog/Samples")

Customcraft is offering free samples and a free catalog of their adorable birth announcements, personalized stationery, handmade baby blankets, and more. Visit their website or call their toll-free number for details. This offer is available to residents of the United States only.

❦ DaimlerChrysler

In the United States, call 877-FIT-4-AKID (Fitting Station Locator)
www.fitforakid.org

More than 80 percent of children are incorrectly restrained in child seats, or the seats are not properly secured in the car. As a result, millions of children are at risk. The Fit for a Kid Program has trained inspectors to help you install your child seats the right way. No matter what kind of car you drive, you can make an appointment at a participating DaimlerChrysler dealer for a free child safety seat inspection, as well as to receive information on car seat safety. Help is available, free of charge, by phone appointment. Call or go online to find the dealer nearest you. This offer is available to residents of the United States only.

✿ Dairy Farmers of Canada
In Canada, call 800-361-4632

Dairy Farmers of Canada offers a free Canada Food Guide Breastfeeding Chart to new or expecting moms. When you call, ask for the order desk to place your order. This offer is available to residents of Canada only.

✿ Del Laboratories (Baby Orajel)
In the United States or Canada, call 800-952-5080
www.orajel.com/baby/baby.html

Call to be put on Baby Orajel's mailing list to receive free coupons and information on Baby Orajel, or fill out the online survey to receive valuable discount coupons and rebates for toothache, teething, and oral care products. This offer is available to residents of the United States and Canada.

✿ Del Monte Nature's Goodness
In the United States, call 800-USA-BABY
www.naturesgoodness.com

Call to receive a free feeding booklet with discount coupons, as well as other free promotional offers from Nature's Goodness. Visit the website to sign up for Del Monte Nature's Goodness special offers mailing list to receive important product updates, information, coupons, and other special offers.

This company has a multiple-birth program for parents of twins, triplets, quadruplets, or more. Ask for details.

These offers are available to residents of the United States only.

❀ **Diaper Genie**
See Playtex Products, Inc.

❀ **Drypers**
See Associated Hygienic Products.

❀ **Earth's Best Baby Food**
See Hain Celestial Group, Inc.

❀ **Evenflo Company, Inc.**
Attn: Multiple Birth Program
1801 Commerce Drive
Piqua, OH 45356
www.evenflo.com

The Evenflo website offers three free brochures to new and expecting parents: a breast-feeding guide, a guide to help with the proper selection and use of car seats, and an Evenflo product catalog.

This company has a multiple-birth program for twins, triplets, and quadruplets. Write to receive free feeding items, including feeding bottles and a baby bib. You can register when the babies are born by sending a copy of the babies' birth certificates. This offer is available to residents of the United States and Canada.

❀ **First Moments Inc.**
Expectant Parents Division
55 Northern Boulevard
Greenvale, NY 11548-1390
In the United States, call 850-474-4142

First Moments is offering a free First Moments Expectant Parent Kit for new or expectant parents! This parent kit, which contains a childbirth planner, samples, coupons, literature, and more, is available through your hospital, doctor's office, or childbirth educator. If you don't receive this free parent kit at the hospital where you will be giving birth to your baby, be sure to ask your nurse, doctor, or other hospital staff about it. This offer is available to residents of the United States only.

Flanders, Inc.
Marketing Services
P.O. Box 5323
Aiken, SC 29804
www.flandersbuttocksointment.com

For two free samples of Flanders Buttocks Ointment for diaper rash, send two loose first-class stamps with your name and address to Flanders. This offer is available to residents of the United States only.

Food Stamp Program
See Chapter 7, "Free Government Resources for New or Expecting Parents," for information on how residents of the United States can receive free food stamps to buy nutritional foods for their family.

Gerber Products Company (U.S.)
In the United States, call 800-4-GERBER
www.gerber.com/special

Call to sign up for Gerber's mailing list to receive coupons for baby food and a free informational booklet. Check out Gerber's website to receive up to $45 (U.S.) in valuable coupons for Gerber products, special offers, samples and more when you join Growing Up Gerber.

This company has a multiple-birth program for parents of twins, triplets, quadruplets, or more. Please send copies of your babies' birth certificates to Gerber at the following address:

Gerber Products Company
Attn: Multiple Birth Program
445 State Street
Fremont, MI 49413

These offers are available to residents of the United States only.

❦ Gerber Products Company (Canada)
In Canada, call 800-4-GERBER
www.gerbercanada.com (click on "Special Offers")

Call to receive coupons for Gerber baby products and a free informational booklet. Check out Gerber's website to sign up to receive even more savings and special offers.

Please note: Gerber baby food is only available in the United States, but Gerber baby products, including breast-feeding products, baby care items, pacifiers, teethers, and drinking cups, are sold in the United States and Canada.

This company has a multiple-birth program for parents of twins, triplets, quadruplets, or more. Please send copies of your babies' birth certificates to Gerber at the following address:

Gerber Products Company
Attn: Multiple Birth Program
445 State Street
Fremont, MI 49413

These offers are available to residents of Canada only.

❦ Growing Family Network
In the United States or Canada, call 888-556-4444 (press #5)
www.growingfamily.com (click on "Network")

Growing Family, a company dedicated to helping families, is the leading in-hospital infant photo service provider in the United States and Canada. Growing Family offers new parents free membership in

the Growing Family Network. As your baby grows from infant to toddler, you will receive new offers and gift packets to meet your child's
new needs from Growing Family and a select group of leading companies. Call or visit the website to register for your free membership. This
offer is available to residents of the United States and Canada.

Gymboree Play and Music

In the United States or Canada, call 800-520-PLAY
www.gymboree.com (click on "Play, Music & Art Classes," then
"Attend a Free Class")

Gymboree offers play classes for children from newborn through
four years of age and music classes for children sixteen months through
four years. Gymboree transforms colorful playscapes, creative activities,
gentle sensory stimulation, and high-energy teachers into a fun-filled
program for parents and children. Call to schedule a free preview class,
or go online to print out a free class coupon. This offer is available to
residents of the United States and Canada.

Hain Celestial Group, Inc. (Earth's Best Baby Food)

In the United States or Canada, call 800-442-4221
www.earthsbest.com (click on "Join the Earth's Best Family")

Earth's Best is the only full line of organic baby food grown without
potentially harmful pesticides, herbicides, or fertilizers. Call to register
to receive a free brochure with money-saving coupons as well as for
information on Earth's Best Baby Food. Residents of the United States
can also register online to join the Earth's Best Family Program to receive
a free brochure and coupons. There are also other great free offers from
Earth's Best:

- Receive a free (plus $1.49 [U.S.] for shipping and handling)
  Sesame Street Let's Eat! Funny Food Songs videotape when you
  purchase two Earth's Best Sesame Street products. Visit the

website for details. This offer is available to residents of the United States only.

- When you send twelve UPCs (universal product codes) from any Earth's Best product, you will receive a free *Guess How Much I Love You* board book. Visit the website for details.
- You can also register at the Earth's Best website to receive a free cereal bowl by sending in ten UPCs from any Earth's Best products. Check the website for details.

(Earth's Best has partnered with Tushies. For further savings, look for the $1.50 [U.S.] off Earth's Best coupons on all Tushies packs.)

These offers are available to residents of the United States and Canada.

H. J. Heinz Company (Canada)
In Canada, call 800-565-2100
www.heinzbaby.com

Since 1991, Canadian parents have helped to raise more than $2 million (Canadian) for the Children's Miracle Network by sending in their Heinz baby labels! Call to participate in the Children's Miracle Network Program. This is a label-saving program where you can collect and send in the labels or box tops from any Heinz baby product. Through the Children's Miracle Network, Heinz will donate 6¢ for each label collected to a local participating children's hospital. Call for further details. Start saving your labels today for a good cause!

Call, or visit the Heinz website to find out about the Heinz Rewards program and how you can receive free toys from Little Tykes by collecting and sending in the Heinz labels for baby food and baby cereal. Sign up online to receive free e-newsletters and other special promotional offers from Heinz for new and expecting parents.

This company has a multiple-birth program for parents of twins, triplets, quadruplets, or more. To receive free baby food and baby cereal, send copies of your babies' birth certificates to Heinz at the following address:

H. J. Heinz Company
Attn: Multiples
90 Sheppard Avenue East
Suite 400
Toronto, ON M2N 7K5

These offers are available to residents of Canada only.

✺ Huggies
See Kimberly-Clark Corporation.

✺ Johnson & Johnson (U.S.)
In the United States, call 800-526-3967
www.JohnsonsBaby.com
www.baby.com

Parents can call to receive a free baby care basics brochure with valuable coupons, as well as to receive occasional mailings with further offers from Johnson & Johnson. Visit the Johnson's Baby website to sign up for a free personalized newsletter and other special offers. When you sign up, you will automatically be entered for a chance to win a diaper bag filled with $50 worth of Johnson's Baby products. There is one winner each month.

This company has a multiple-birth program for parents of twins, triplets, quadruplets, or more. Ask for details.

These offers are available to residents of the United States only.

✺ Johnson & Johnson/McNeil Consumer Healthcare (Canada)
In Canada, call 800-361-8068
www.jnjcanada.com
www.mcneilcanada.com

Johnson & Johnson has teamed up with McNeil Consumer Healthcare (makers of Motrin and Tylenol) to offer a free New Parent's Pack to new and expecting parents. This New Parent's Pack is filled with coupons, free product samples, baby care information, and health care information from Johnson & Johnson and McNeil Consumer Healthcare. Call Johnson & Johnson to receive your free New Parent's Pack.

This company has a multiple-birth program for parents of twins, triplets, quadruplets, or more. Ask for details.

This offer is available to residents of Canada only.

Kimberly-Clark Corporation (Huggies)

In the United States or Canada, call 800-544-1847
www.huggies.com/na/offers/index.asp
www.kimberly-clark.com

Call to be added to the Huggies mailing list for new or expectant parents. You will receive coupons for Huggies diapers, baby wipes, and other promotional items and free samples that are being offered at the time. Huggies will also send out occasional mailings and coupons at the different stages of your baby's development. You can also register online to join the Huggies Special Offers mailing list to receive money-saving coupons and other special offers, enter to win a year's supply of Huggies products, receive the Parentstages.com e-newsletter, and more. Visit the website for details.

This company has a multiple-birth program for parents of twins, triplets, quadruplets, or more. To receive a one-time gift of coupons, send copies of your babies' birth certificates or birth announcement to:

Kimberly-Clark Corporation
Department QMB
P.O. Box 2020
Neenah, WI 54957-2020

In Canada, write:

Kimberly-Clark, Inc.
Department QMB
50 Burnhamthorpe Road West
Mississauga, ON L5B 3Y5

These offers are available to residents of the United States and Canada.

Kushies

Kushies Baby
555 Barton Street
Stoney Creek, ON L8E 5S1
In the United States or Canada, call 800-841-5330
www.kushies.com; www.kooshies.com

Parents can enter their adorable new baby in Kushies free "Baby of the Month" contest for a chance to receive $75 worth of Kushies products! To be eligible, send a photo of your baby using or wearing Kushies products to the address listed above. Visit the website for further details. This offer is available to residents of the United States and Canada.

Lansinoh Laboratories, Inc.

In the United States or Canada, call 800-292-4794

Call to receive a free sample of soothing and protecting breast-feeding cream made with pure lanolin. This offer is available to residents of the United States and Canada.

Little Remedies Products

In the United States, call 800-754-8853
www.littleremedies.com

"We Make It All Better," claims Little Remedies Products, by providing safe, gentle relief of the common discomforts experienced by infants and children, without the addition of harmful preservatives or unnecessary additives. To receive valuable coupons and information from Little Remedies, call or go online to view the complete product line and special offers. This offer is available to residents of the United States only.

❧ Little Tykes

In the United States or Canada, call 800-321-0183

Call Little Tykes to be added to their mailing list to receive free promotional items and a Little Tykes catalog. This offer is available to residents of the United States and Canada.

❧ Mead Johnson Nutritionals (U.S.)

In the United States, call 800-BABY-123
www.enfamil.com

Call, or register online to take part in the free Enfamil Family Beginnings program and receive up to $250 in gifts and discounts. Visit www.enfamil.com/enfamil8.html and print out the page to pack in your suitcase. Give it to your nurse at the hospital when your baby arrives to receive a free Enfamil LIPIL Smart Bag filled with samples, educational materials, critical safety information, and a hearing health checklist, compliments of the Enfamil Family of Formulas. (This offer is available at participating hospitals.)

This company has a multiple-birth program for parents of twins, triplets, quadruplets, or more. Ask for details.

These offers are available to residents of the United States only.

❧ Mead Johnson Nutritionals (Canada)

In Canada, call 800-361-6323
www.enfamil.ca/en/steps/program.html

Residents of Canada can call or register online to receive discounts on baby formula and to join the Enfamil First Connections Program. When you join the Enfamil First Connections Program, here's what you will receive:

- A keepsake box with a free product sample and coupons, along with informational brochures.
- Three booklets to help you make informed decisions about the best nutritional care for the growth and development of you and

your baby. Each booklet comes with quick and easy reference cards to hang on your fridge. These reference cards can also be used as flash cards to entertain and stimulate your baby; they contain information on subjects such as the stages of labor and ways to soothe your crying baby.

- A free nutritional information book titled *Nourishing Your Baby.*

This company has a multiple-birth program for parents of twins, triplets, quadruplets, or more. Ask for details.

These offers are available to residents of Canada only.

✿ McNeil Consumer & Specialty Pharmaceuticals
In the United States, call 800-962-5357 (press #5)
www.tylenol.com
www.motrin.com

Call to receive coupons for Infants' or Children's Tylenol or for Children's Motrin, a medical recording booklet for your child, or free promotional offers from Johnson & Johnson. This offer is available to residents of the United States only.

✿ Milupa
In Canada, call 866-335-9080

Call Milupa to receive a free baby spoon, a "Baby in Car" bumper sticker, a discount coupon for money off Milupa infant cereal, as well as a free nutrition guide. This offer is available to residents of Canada only.

✿ Mom Pack
See Preciouskids.org.

✿ Mother-Ease
In the United States or Canada, call 800-416-1475
www.mother-ease.com

Mother-Ease is a manufacturer of environmentally friendly, reusable cotton diapers, as well as cloth diapering products. Call Mother-Ease for their free pamphlet, including fabric samples, as well as a special introductory offer. This offer is available to residents of the United States and Canada.

🐾 Mother of Eden

In the United States or Canada, call 866-DRY-BABY
www.fuzzibunz.com

Fuzzi Bunz are rash-free, leak-free, waterproof cloth diapers by Mother of Eden. Call to request a free information pack and free new mom gift. This offer is available to residents of the United States and Canada.

🐾 National Institute of Child Health and Human Development

In the United States, call 800-370-2943
www.nichd.nih.gov/sids/sids.cfm

The Back to Sleep Campaign is a program that provides information on SIDS (sudden infant death syndrome) and the importance of placing healthy babies on their backs to sleep. Residents of the United States can call to receive free SIDS safety stickers, a magnet, a door hanger reminding you to put your baby to sleep on his or her back, and a brochure that offers information about SIDS and how to protect your infant. Residents of the United States or Canada can order online.

🐾 Nature's One

In the United States, call 614-898-9758 (press #2) (sorry, not a toll-
    free number)
www.naturesone.com/sample.htm

Baby's Only Organic pediatric infant formula is made with organic ingredients. Call for a free sample of either the dairy-based or soy-based infant formula.

For every twenty-four proof-of-purchase seals that you collect and save from Nature's One products, you will be sent a coupon for two free units of the same product. Click on "Rebate" at the website for instructions on how you can receive a free mail-in rebate. You also have the option of pledging your free product to Feed the Children. Check the Feed the Children website (www.feedthechildren.org) for details. Nature's One will donate a portion of its after-tax profits in the form of money and product to help support Feed the Children.

These offers are available to residents of the United States only.

Nestlé Canada
In Canada, call 800-387-5536
www.nestle-baby.ca

Call, or register online to join the Nestlé Baby Program and receive a free subscription to the *Nestlé Baby Magazine* for expecting and new moms. The magazine provides information, advice, and support for you and your growing baby—from nutrition tips to parenting insights and everything in between. Along with your free magazine subscription, you will receive valuable coupons, free samples of infant formula and baby cereal (if you choose), plus information and savings on special products for new parents.

This company also has a multiple-birth program where parents of multiples will receive a free case of the infant formula of their choice, including Good Start or Alsoy infant formula.

Register as soon as you are expecting to receive the greatest benefits from this program. Please call the toll-free number for details on how to register. These offers are available to residents of Canada only.

Nestlé Infant Nutrition (U.S.)
In the United States, call 800-242-5200
www.verybestbaby.com

Call to sign up for The Very Best Baby to receive a free subscription to *The Very Best Baby Collection*, including free money-saving checks for Nestlé Infant Nutrition products, an exclusive baby keepsake, and more.

You can also register online to join The Very Best Baby at the website listed above. When you register online to join, you can choose to receive an assortment of free benefits, including a free subscription to *The Very Best Baby Collection*, e-mail pregnancy and baby updates, and more.

Visit www.verybestbaby.com/content/backpack.asp to receive a free Very Best Baby backpack, a stylish and practical diaper bag filled with tons of free gifts for mom and baby, including a *Mommy and Me* music CD, Munchkin baby bottle, photo album, and more. Simply print out the online gift certificate and ask the nurse for your complimentary Very Best Baby backpack at the hospital when your baby arrives. (This offer is available at participating hospitals.)

This company also has a multiple-birth program where parents of twins, triples, quadruplets, or more can receive free cans of infant formula, a free subscription to *The Very Best Baby* magazine, and money-saving checks for infant nutrition products. Copies of your babies' birth certificates are required. Call for details on how you can sign up for this program.

These offers are available to residents of the United States only.

New Beginnings

In the United States or Canada, call 800-573-2049
www.yournewbeginnings.com

Call to receive a free New Beginnings birth announcement brochure and product samples. This offer is available to residents of the United States and Canada.

Ocean Spray Cranberries, Inc.

Consumer Affairs Department
One Ocean Spray Drive
Lakeville-Middleboro, MA 02349
In the United States or Canada, call 800-662-3263
U.S. website: www.oceanspray.com
Canadian website: www.oceanspray.ca

Call or write to be added to Ocean Spray's mailing list to receive a free recipe booklet and product coupons for Ocean Spray products. Include a copy of your baby's birth certificate with your written request to Ocean Spray.

This company has a multiple-birth program for parents of twins, triplets, quadruplets, or more. Send copies of your babies' birth certificates to the address listed above to receive a free recipe booklet and product coupons. These offers are available to residents of the United States and Canada.

❧ Option Line (National Pregnancy Helpline)
In the United States and Canada, call 800-395-HELP
www.optionline.org

Option Line is a twenty-four-hour, toll-free help line that supports more than eight hundred pregnancy centers across the United States and Canada. You can call Option Line with your pregnancy-related questions and concerns or to receive practical assistance and support. Option Line will refer you to the pregnancy center nearest you. Residents of the United States and Canada can call Option Line to receive a free pregnancy test.

❧ Our Kids, Inc.
In the United States, call 877-909-7684
In Canada, call 561-741-3344 (sorry, not a toll-free number)
www.baby-be-safe.com

Our Kids offers 100-percent-cotton crib sheets that stay secure to crib mattresses and are easy for an adult to change. In addition to a flat secure crib sheet, Our Kids offers Baby-Be-Safe crib sheets that come with an elevation wedge. They are the only sheets on the market today that come with an elevation sleep wedge that stays securely in place. These sheets are recommended by pediatricians for their safety and medical benefits. When you call to order a free brochure, you will also be sent a free emergency wipe board, as well as fabric samples for Baby-

Be-Safe crib sheets. This offer is available to residents of the United States only.

✿ OxiClean Baby

In the United States, call 888-414-2219
www.oxicleanbaby.com

OxiClean Baby is a baby stain remover that removes stains—such as baby food, juice, and diaper leakage—without harsh chemicals. Call for a free sample. This offer is available to residents of the United States only.

✿ Pampers

See Procter & Gamble.

✿ Parents Canada

In Canada, call 416-537-2604 (sorry, not a toll-free number)
www.parentscanada.com (click on "Join Now")

Parents Canada has been Canada's most trusted provider of parenting information for over fifty years. Call, or sign up online to receive a free subscription to *Parents Canada Magazine*. Visit the website to receive access to their site's interactive features, including information on pregnancy, labor and birth, caring for your baby, and more. When you enter the Parents Canada Baby Sweepstakes, you will receive a free baby care savings coupon pack. This offer is available to residents of Canada only.

✿ Pfizer Inc. (Desitin)

In the United States, call 800-223-0182 (press #1)

Pfizer makes Desitin diaper rash ointment and other baby and family-related products. Parents can call Pfizer to request a free "New Mother's Kit" with valuable coupons, baby product samples, and informational brochures. This offer is available to residents of the United States only.

❧ **Playtex Products, Inc.**
Playtex Products
75 Commerce Drive
Allendale, NJ 07401
In Canada, call 800-387-1300
www.playtexbaby.com (click on "Receive Our Newsletter")

Call Playtex to join the Joy of Feeding Program and receive a free informational brochure, Playtex product coupons, and more. This offer is available to residents of Canada only. Sign up online to receive the Playtex.com Baby Newsletter, free samples, and special offers. This offer is available to residents of the United States and Canada.

This company has a multiple-birth program for parents of twins, triplets, quadruplets, or more. Please send copies of your babies' birth certificates to the address listed above. This offer is available to residents of the United States and Canada.

❧ **Playtex Products, Inc. (Diaper Genie)**
Playtex Products
20 Troy Road
Whippany, NJ 07981
In the United States or Canada, call 800-843-6430
www.playtexbaby.com

Parents of multiples can call or write to join the Multiple Birth Sample Program. Send your name, your mailing address, and copies of your babies' birth certificates or birth announcement. (Your request must be sent before your babies turn three months of age.) This offer is available to residents of the United States and Canada.

❧ **Polly Klaas Foundation**
In the United States or Canada, call 800-587-4357
www.pollyklaas.org (click on "Child Safety Kit")

The Polly Klaas Foundation, which aids in the search for missing children, is dedicated to educating parents on protecting their children from child abduction, as well as other safety issues. Call for a free Child Safety Kit with fingerprint and DNA capabilities. There is no fee for the ID kits; however, a donation of $3 is appreciated to help cover shipping and handling costs. You can register to receive one kit for each child in your family. This free kit includes the following:

- *Polly Klaas Foundation History and Activities*
- *Your Child . . . the Truth*
- *Child Identification Booklet*
- *Child Safety: Important Information You Should Know*
- *Parental Abductions . . . the Truth*
- *Runaways . . . the Truth*
- *Internet Abduction . . . the Truth*

Safety kits cost the foundation approximately 76¢ to produce and 78¢ (U.S.) to mail. While the foundation continues to take requests, please be aware that it receives no government funding and the organization exists solely because of donations. This offer is available to residents of the United States and Canada.

Preciouskids.org

Precious Kids
Coupon Packs
P.O. Box 271
Banks, OR 97106
www.preciouskids.org/mompack.html

Order your free Mom Pack filled with flyers, coupons, and samples from several moms with home-based businesses. The pack is absolutely free; however, because of the size and weight of the pack, please send four postage stamps to cover the postage costs. You can also order your free Mom Pack online. This offer is available to residents of the United States only.

❀ **Procter & Gamble (Pampers) (U.S.)**
   In the United States, call 800-543-0480
   www.pampers.com (click on "Register")

Visit the website to join Pampers' free mailing list and receive a free welcome kit from Pampers filled with samples and coupons for Pampers' products, as well as to receive the free "Parent Pages" monthly newsletter. All members will automatically be entered into Pampers Welcome Sweepstakes for a chance to win a year's supply of free Pampers' products, as well as special offers from other Procter & Gamble brands. Pampers will also send out occasional mailings and coupons at the different stages of your baby's development.

This company has a multiple-birth program for parents of twins, triplets, quadruplets, or more. To receive a free one-time gift offer from Pampers, call to sign up at the number listed above, or mail your name and address, along with copies of your babies' birth certificates (or verification of birth on your doctor's letterhead stationery), to:

   Pampers Multiple Birth Offer
   The Procter & Gamble Company
   P.O. Box 599
   Cincinnati, OH 45201

These offers are available to residents of the United States only.

❀ **Procter & Gamble (Pampers) (Canada)**
   In Canada, call 800-726-7377
   www.pampers.ca (click on "Register")

Visit the website to join Pampers' free mailing list and receive a free welcome kit from Pampers filled with samples and coupons for Pampers' products, as well as to receive the free "Parent Pages" monthly newsletter. All members will automatically be entered into Pampers Welcome Sweepstakes for a chance to win a year's supply of free Pampers' products, as well as special offers from other Procter & Gamble brands. Pampers will also send out occasional mailings and coupons at the different stages of your baby's development.

This company has a multiple-birth program for parents of twins, triplets, quadruplets, or more. To receive a free one-time gift offer from Pampers, call to sign up at the number listed earlier, or mail your name and address, along with copies of your babies' birth certificates (or verification of birth on your doctor's letterhead stationery), to:

Pampers Multiple Birth Offer
The Procter & Gamble Company
P.O. Box 355, Station A
Toronto, ON M5W 1C5

These offers are available to residents of Canada only.

❧ Procter & Gamble Brand Saver

In the United States or Canada, call 800-668-0150
U.S. website: www.brandsaver.com (click on "Offers & Promotions")
Canadian website: www.brandsaver.ca (click on "Offers & Promotions")

Call, or sign up online to receive free samples, as well as money off P & G products, including Pampers, Tide, Crest, Mr. Clean, Always, Pantene, Olay, Tampax, Downy, Puffs, and Charmin. Over $40 in coupon savings! This offer is available to residents of the United States and Canada. Residents of Canada can visit www.s-mag.ca to sign up to receive Procter & Gamble's free *S-Magazine* online, a magazine to help you save time and money, as well as a monthly e-mail newsletter packed with samples and savings.

❧ PureTouch Skin Care

PureTouch
6280 Artesia Boulevard
Buena Park, CA 90620
Attn: Customer Care
In the United States, call 866-TUSH-WIPES (866-887-4947)
www.puretouchskincare.com

Tush Wipes for Babies are flushable moist wipes that help prevent diaper rash. An alternative to dry bathroom tissue, they are gentle and soothing on baby's skin. For a free sample, send a self-addressed stamped envelope
to the address listed earlier. Be sure to include the name of the product you
would like to sample, "Tush Wipes for Babies," in your letter to them, as well
as your first and last name, address, city, state, zip code, and telephone number. This offer is available to residents of the United States only.

❦ Ringling Bros. and Barnum & Bailey Circus

Baby Program
Feld Entertainment, Inc.
Attn: Customer Relations
8607 Westwood Center Drive
Vienna, VA 22182
www.ringling.com/offers

If you love the circus, here's something you won't want to miss! The
Ringling Bros. and Barnum & Bailey Circus is giving every newborn
(twelve months and under) his or her first ticket to "The Greatest Show
on Earth" absolutely free! Write for one free ticket per child, or fill out
the online form to request your free ticket. In your written request,
please include your name, your home address and phone number, your
child's first name and birth date, together with a photocopy of your
child's birth certificate. (Tickets are good for an unlimited time.) This
offer is available to residents of the United States only.

Parents of multiples can request free tickets by mailing copies of
their babies' birth certificates to Ringling Bros. and Barnum & Bailey
Circus.

❦ Sassy, Inc.

In the United States, call 800-323-6336
www.sassybaby.com

Sassy offers educational and stimulating products for your baby. Call
to receive a free product brochure, a free copy of Sassy's sleep brochure

Sweet Dreams for Baby and You: A Guide to Helping Baby Establish Healthy Sleep Habits, and a free pacifier. Sassy's product brochure contains five "Buy 1, Get 1 Free" offers for parents of twins, triplets, quadruplets, or more. When parents of multiples buy one of these five infant products listed in the brochure, they will be sent an identical item, free of charge. New parents are advised to call Sassy during the last trimester of their pregnancy, as copies of their babies' birth certificates are required. These offers are available to residents of the United States only.

✿ Similac Advance Welcome Addition Club (Canada)

P.O. Box 130
Station Pointe Claire
Pointe Claire, QC H9R 9Z9
In Canada, call 800-518-CLUB
www.abbott.ca/eng/nutrition/#

Call, write, or sign up online to join the Similac Advance Welcome Addition Club to receive coupons and free samples of Similac and other infant formulas, a free gift or sample kit for your baby, and the *Growing with Similac Advance* magazine. This company will also send you occasional mailings with information on your baby's growth and development. This offer is available to residents of Canada only.

✿ Similac Welcome Addition Club (U.S.)

In the United States, call 800-BABYLINE
www.welcomeaddition.com (click on "Join the Club")

Call or go online to join the Similac Welcome Addition Club. Member benefits may include money-saving discounts, free samples of Similac Infant Formulas, periodic newsletters containing expert pregnancy and parenting advice, or other gifts. This offer is available to residents of the United States only.

❦ **Snow Pharmaceuticals, LLC (Snow Balm)**
P.O. Box 29
Selbyville, DE 19975
www.snowbalm.com/sampler.htm

For a free sample of Snow Balm diaper rash ointment, send two first-class stamps to Snow Pharmaceuticals. Also send your name, address, e-mail address, and phone number, as well as the birth dates of children still in diapers. When sending for your sample, please mention that you saw their listing in *Free Stuff for Baby!* Be sure to print your information. This offer is available for a limited time and is only available to residents of the United States. (To be sure of the availability of the current offer, visit the website.)

❦ **Spatone**
In the United States or Canada, call 888-855-2739
www.spatone.com

Spatone Iron+ is a 100 percent natural iron supplement that provides enough iron to meet your increased need during pregnancy and breast-feeding. Call for a free sample. This offer is available to residents of the United States and Canada.

❦ **Spiffies Dental Wipes**
www.drraysproducts.com

Spiffies Dental Wipes are infant cleansing wipes that offer an easy way to clean your baby's mouth and gums. For a free product sample, send a standard self-addressed stamped envelope to:

Dr. Rays Products
3305 North Swan Road, #109
PMB 431
Tucson, AZ 85712

This offer is available to residents of the United States only.

❦ State of Virginia (Child Safety Seat Program)

In the United States, call 800-732-8333

www.safetyseatva.org (click on "Low Income Safety Seat Program")

Through its Child Safety Seat Program, the Virginia Department of Health provides free child safety seats to qualifying low-income families in the state of Virginia. More than seven thousand seats are provided each year through funding from the Child Restraint Special Device Fund and are distributed through local health departments.

To qualify for a free child safety seat, applicant must be a legal resident of Virginia; must be eligible for Medicaid; and must be a parent, legal guardian, or foster parent of the child, or must be, at the earliest, in the last trimester of pregnancy. Recipient is also required to attend a safety seat installation and use class. Check out the website or call for further information and details on how you can receive a free child safety seat.

For those residing outside the state of Virginia, some hospitals and health departments provide new moms with free infant car seats upon giving birth to their new baby at the hospital. Call the hospital where you will be giving birth to see if they have a similar program available to expecting moms.

❦ Stork Grams

In the United States, call 800-268-5197

www.storkgrams.com (click on "Catalog & Sample Requests")

Visit the Stork Grams website, or call the toll-free number to request free samples and a free catalog filled with terrific birth announcements, candy wrappers, and more. You can choose up to four products to sample for free. This offer is available to residents of the United States only.

❦ Stork's Choice Disposable Diaper Service

In the United States, call 877-67-STORK

www.storkschoice.com/sample.asp (click on "Order Sample Pack")

Stork's Choice offers a free sample package containing three Stork's Choice premium disposable diapers or two Stork's Choice premium training pants. There is no charge for the samples, but there is a shipping and handling fee of $2.99. To receive a sample package, fill out the online form or call. This offer is available to residents of the United States only.

❀ Toys "R" Us

In the United States, call 800-TOYSRUS

www.toysrusinc.com

Call to be added to the Babies "R" Us and Toys "R" Us mailing list to receive free coupons, as well as a catalog twice a year from Babies "R" Us. This offer is available to residents of the United States only. Babies "R" Us and Toys "R" Us also have a baby registry where you can register for your baby shower. Visit a Babies "R" Us or Toys "R" Us store or go online to register. (For further details see "Drop-In Freebies" in Chapter 3, "Free Stuff from Stores.")

❀ Transport Canada

In Canada, call 800-333-0371

www.tc.gc.ca/roadsafety (click on "Child Safety")

Transport Canada offers a free entertaining video, *Car Time 1-2-3-4*, and its companion booklet, *Keep Kids Safe*, to help parents properly use and install a child seat in a motor vehicle. The video shows how and when to use rear-facing infant seats, forward-facing child seats, booster seats, and seat belts. An information guide on how to install and use child restraint systems is included in this package. You can request the free video and booklet by calling, or visit the website to view it online. You can also call Transport Canada for more information on child car seat safety. This offer is available to residents of Canada only.

❀ Triaminic Clinic

In the United States, call 800-KIDS-987

Call for a free Triaminic "House Call Kit" with newsletter, Selector Wheel, emergency contact magnet, coupons, samples, and more. This offer is available to residents of the United States only.

❦ Tushies

In the United States, call 800-344-6379

www.tushies.com

Tushies offers a wide assortment of diapers and baby products online. Call to request a free Tushies diaper sample. Tushies is also offering a free Tushies.com tote bag with your first Tushies or Tendercare Club order. Check out the website or call for further details. (This offer is available for a limited time only.) Tushies has a free diaper club where you will receive better prices on Tushies baby products and convenient, automatic delivery every three to six weeks. Call or check the website for details. These offers are available to residents of the United States only.

❦ Welcome Wagon

www.welcomewagon.ca/en/baby/signup/baby_bl.php

www.babystages.ca/en/nbr_en.php

Welcome Wagon is a Canadian-owned free greeting service. If you are a new or expecting mom, Welcome Wagon will greet you with a friendly visit, providing you with free coupons, brochures, and gifts for your baby, as well as a complimentary copy of *Baby Stages* magazine. Call the nearest Welcome Wagon to have a representative contact you. (Welcome Wagon is listed in the white pages in your local telephone book.) You can also fill out Welcome Wagon's online form to have a representative contact you. In order to receive your free gifts from Welcome Wagon, you must be expecting or have a newborn. This offer is available to residents of Canada only.

❦ Welcome Wagon Baby Shower

www.welcomewagon.ca/en (click on "Upcoming Shows")

A Welcome Wagon Baby Shower is a free group function for expecting moms that is held at various locations throughout Canada. This fun and educational baby shower provides educational speakers, displays, shows, and more for the expecting mom. To register to receive a free invitation to a Welcome Wagon Baby Shower for expectant mothers, fill out the online form at the website or call the Welcome Wagon nearest you. (Welcome Wagon is listed in the white pages in your local telephone book.) To find out when a Welcome Wagon Baby Shower will be held in your area, visit the website to view the various locations, dates, and times. This offer is available to residents of Canada only.

❦ Weleda Newborn Kit
In the United States, call 800-241-1030

Weleda offers free product samples intermittently throughout the year. Call for information on current offers. You can also call to receive a free Weleda catalog featuring quality baby care and personal care products. This offer is available to residents of the United States only.

❦ White House
Greetings Office
1600 Pennsylvania Avenue NW
Washington, DC 20500

The president of the United States would like to welcome your newest arrival to the world with a special signed congratulatory announcement. Simply send a copy of your baby's birth announcement or write a note with your baby's date of birth to the White House.

❦ WIC (Women, Infants, and Children)
See Chapter 7, "Free Government Resources for New or Expecting Parents," to find out how low-income families in the United States can receive—free from the government—nutritious foods, infant formula, and cereal during their baby's first years.

❦ Window Covering Safety Council

In the United States or Canada, call 800-506-4636

www.windowcoverings.org (click on "Order Free Repair Kit")

A number of children have strangled in the loops of window blind and curtain cords. Be sure that your blinds do not have looped cords. To assist in this safety precaution, the Window Covering Safety Council offers free childproofing kits to help prevent cord accidents related to window blinds. The organization will provide free safety tassels, cord stops, and tie-down devices, as well as instructions on how to install these safety devices.

Call, or visit the website for details. This offer is available to residents of the United States and Canada.

❦ Wyeth-Ayerst Canada Inc.

In Canada, call 800-387-8647 (ext. 7080)

Parents can call Wyeth to request free money-saving coupons for Children's Advil and Children's Dimetapp. This offer is available to residents of Canada only.

❦ Wyeth Pharmaceuticals

Product Quality

P.O. Box 26609

Richmond, VA 23261-6609

In the United States, call 888-797-5638

Call or write to be placed on Wyeth's mailing list to receive free coupons for discounts on Wyeth products, including Children's Advil, Dimetapp, and Anbesol. This offer is available to residents of the United States only.

This company has a multiple-birth program offering free product coupons for Wyeth products to parents of twins, triplets, quadruplets, or more. Ask for details.

❧ Xttrium Laboratories

415 West Pershing Road
Chicago, IL 60609
In the United States or Canada, call 800-587-3721
www.xttrium.com

Call to receive free trial-size samples of DRC, a fragrance-free, water-repellant diaper rash cream, together with a mail-in rebate coupon. This offer is available to residents of the United States and Canada.

2

Baby Freebies on the Net

Cyber freak, cyber geek—call me what you like, but I just can't seem to get enough of the Internet! With a few clicks of the mouse, you can chat with other parents from around the world, get up-to-date on the latest baby products, swap baby food recipes, and read about other parents' birth experiences. Literally anything and everything to do with babies and parenting can be found on the World Wide Web.

There are hundreds, if not thousands, of baby websites on the Internet, and I have been to many of them, surfing the Net until the wee hours of the morning to find the best online deals for you and your baby.

So for all of you computer-savvy parents out there, here is a listing of some great websites that offer even more terrific freebies!

If you don't own a computer, maybe you can borrow one from a friend or get online at your local library. Most libraries now have computers that you can use free of charge. These sites have some great online offers that you won't want to miss!

Free Product Samples, Coupons, and More

The following fabulous websites list tons of different freebies that parents can quickly and conveniently sign up for online, including free music CDs and DVDs, baby formula, discount coupons, and baby product samples and gifts.

When you're ready to start potty training your little one, don't forget to check out Charmin's free potty-training kit. It's adorable!

❧ Amphion Communications
www.2bparent.com/calendar.htm

This website offers a free fetal development calendar where you can find out when your baby will acquire new abilities. This offer is available to residents of the United States only.

❧ Anbesol
www.anbesol.com/teething/chart.asp

Visit the Anbesol website to receive a free printable baby tooth chart to keep track of when each of your baby's first teeth appear.

❧ Avent America
www.aventamerica.com/support/requestbrochures.asp

Avent America, a company that offers award-winning infant feeding products, is offering a free breast-feeding guide and sample to new and expecting parents. To receive their free offer, visit the website to fill out the online form. This offer is available to residents of the United States and Canada.

❧ Babies Online Automated Birth Announcement System
www.babiesonline.com

Show off your new bundle of joy to friends and family around the world with Babies Online automated birth announcement system. Your baby can have her own Web page, complete with pictures, music, your choice of background style, and your own guest book. It only takes a few minutes to create—and it's free!

Babies Online Pregnancy Planner
www.babiesonline.com/pregnancy/planner/content.asp

Babies Online offers a free pregnancy planner that calculates the biologically preferred days for getting pregnant. If you are hoping for a girl or a boy, the planner also suggests some actions that may influence the sex of the child, based on scientific research.

Baby BumbleBee
www.babybumblebee.com/v2/pages/freebies.cfm

Baby BumbleBee provides parents with educationally appropriate materials, including educational videos, for infants and toddlers. The website offers an assortment of valuable teaching tools for your baby that you can print out for free. Alphabet posters are colorful posters that can be printed out and placed around your baby's room to help teach the alphabet. Number posters can be printed out to help teach number recognition and counting. Bee Smart Baby Vocabulary Builder Flashcards can be used to enhance your infant's language acquisition. The Infant Safety Checklist will provide you with information for making your home safe for your baby. Topics include kitchen and bathroom safety, choking, poisoning, hazardous items, electrical hazards, and car and crib safety. The page called "Tips for Promoting Speech and Language Development" has great ideas to help infants and toddlers in these areas.

BabyCenter
www.babycenter.com

The BabyCenter website offers a free membership where you will receive weekly development updates, as well as free online birth announcements. This website also includes an easy-to-follow milestone chart, advice on when to call the doctor, chat rooms, an immunization scheduler, and more.

❦ Baby Einstein
www.babyeinstein.com/fitpregnancy
www.babyeinstein.com (click on "View Our Product Demos")

Baby Einstein offers a wide assortment of interactive developmental products for babies, including DVDs, videos, music CDs, books and toys, and more. Visit the website to request a free Baby Einstein DVD or CD music sampler in the mail. This offer is available to residents of the United States only.

To join the Baby Einstein mailing list to receive e-mail news, product updates, and special announcements, visit the following website: www.babyeinstein.com (click on "What's New," then "Join Mailing List"). The mailing list is available to residents of the United States and Canada. You can also visit their website to view their free video and audio product demo samples online.

❦ Baby Orajel
www.orajel.com/baby/index.html

Visit the website to find out how you can receive a manufacturer's mail-in refund on the purchase of any Orajel or Baby Orajel product for toothache, teething, or oral care needs. This offer is available to residents of the United States only.

❦ BabyPlans
www.babyplans.com/newadditionsmenu.html (click on "Submit a New Birth Announcement")

At BabyPlans you can announce the birth of your new bundle of joy by creating a free home page for the world to see!

❦ Baby's Dream Furniture

www.babysdream.com/marketing/GrowthChart.asp

Visit the Baby's Dream Furniture website to view their adorable baby furniture or to receive a free growth chart to help keep track of your baby's height. This offer is available to residents of the United States only.

❦ Baby Whisperer International

www.babywhisperer.com (click on "Hogg Watch")

Parents can visit the Baby Whisperer website to sample and rate new baby products for free. Visit the website for details. This offer is available to residents of the United States and Canada.

❦ BabyZone

www.babyzone.com (click on "Free Stuff")

Register online to receive free stuff, including coupons and catalogs for new or expecting parents. Just for fun, try to predict the sex of your baby using this free online Chinese lunar calendar (www.babyzone .com/babynames/chinese.asp). It is believed that this chart has been proven by thousands of people and is 99 percent accurate!

❦ Bama Babies & Birthdays

www.bamababiesandbirthdays.com (click on "Free Goodie Bag")

Looking for big, bold, colorful yard signs to announce the birth of your new baby? Bama Babies & Birthdays offers an assortment of colorful signs, including storks, moons, and cows. They also offer an assortment of affordable baby gifts. Visit the website to order a free goodie bag packed full of coupons, specials offers, and information. A small postage fee of $1.95 is required to have the item shipped to you. This offer is available to residents of the United States only.

❧ Beech-Nut
www.beechnut.com/bib

When you sign up for Beech-Nut's monthly newsletter, they will send you information customized to your baby's age, money-saving coupons and offers, and a free baby bib. This offer is available to residents of the United States only.

❧ BellyCast.com
www.bellycast.com

Arbonne International offers botanically based skin care products for babies, including hair and body wash, herbal diaper rash cream, and more. Visit the BellyCast website to request a free baby care sample from Arbonne International. This offer is available to residents of the United States only.

❧ Born to Love
www.borntolove.com/catalogues.html (click on "Choose Your Free Newsletters")

The Born to Love website offers an assortment of baby newsletters that you can receive free via e-mail, such as *Baby Marketplace*, *This Baby of Mine*, and *Parentsline News*. This offer is available to residents of the United States only.

❧ BreastMilk.com
www.breastmilk.com (click on "Breastfeeding Tracker")

If you're breast-feeding or planning to breast-feed, BreastMilk.com offers great breast-feeding products, including breast pumps, breast milk storage products, and breast-feeding aids. Visit the website to receive a free downloadable breast-feeding tracker to keep track of your baby's breast-feeding schedule.

❧ Bright Beginnings
www.brightbeginnings.com (click on "Customer Club")

Bright Beginnings is a DHA-enhanced infant formula that provides nutrients at levels similar to those in breast milk. When you register online to join the free "Customer Club," you will receive a Membership Pak containing a free $7.50 voucher for Bright Beginnings Baby Formula, a free sample of Bright Beginnings Baby Formula, free Coupon Paks, and a free Bright Beginnings monthly newsletter. When you save and send in your Proof of Purchase labels (UPC code) from any Bright Beginnings product, they'll send you a free Bright Beginnings Stork Doll and a $5 Coupon Pak. Additional coupons and offers will be mailed to you on a regular basis. Check out the website for details. This offer is available to residents of the United States only.

❧ Bryce Foster Corporation (Fresh Sacks)
www.freshsacks.com/babycontact.html

Fresh Sacks are convenient diaper disposal bags that are designed to eliminate diaper odor. Visit their website to receive a free five-bag sample pack and a manufacturer's rebate. Fresh Sacks are available at Walgreen's nationwide. This offer is available to residents of the United States only.

❧ Build a Baby Book
www.buildababybook.com

At the Build a Baby Book website you can build an online baby book with features that enable you to upload photos to your child's photo album, a daily journal, list of first year developments, and more. Visit www.buildababybook.com/241coupon.jpg to print out a "buy one, get one free" coupon.

❧ Canadian Parents Online Baby Food Recipes
www.canadianparents.com/canadacooks (click on "Baby Food")

This website contains some great, nutritious baby food recipes that you can make at home in your food processor or blender.

Charmin
www.charmin.com/en_us/pages/pt.shtml

Visit the website to sign up to receive a free potty-training kit. This fun and adorable potty-training kit will help you teach your child proper bathroom habits. Each kit includes a free "Ready . . . Set . . . Go!" poster to hang up in your bathroom as a reminder for your little one, stickers to match to each of the steps in the poster, a cute storybook, a picture frame magnet, and a roll ruler. The Charmin roll ruler hangs on the toilet roll to teach kids exactly how much tissue to use. Once your child has successfully completed potty training, you can recognize his or her achievement with a diploma from "Charmin University." This offer is available to residents of the United States and Canada.

Chart Jungle
www.chartjungle.com/pottycharts.html

Chart Jungle offers free potty time charts and certificates for completing potty training for boys and girls. You can use stickers or markers on these adorable potty charts to mark off the days of the week. There are numerous other free charts that you can print out at Chart Jungle as well, including bedtime charts with bedtime reminders, free award charts, "Mom, I'm Bored" charts with activity suggestions, and chore charts.

Childavenue
www.childavenue.com (click on "Family Corner")

This parenting website offers a free printable Potty Training Reward chart for your child.

❦ ClubMom

www.clubmom.com

ClubMom is the national membership organization for moms. By bringing together millions of moms, ClubMom can get special rewards, savings, and status for its members from America's best companies. ClubMom membership is as good as it sounds. No fees. No catch. Just tons of value for moms. This offer is available to residents of the United States only.

❦ Computer Mommy

www.computermommy.com/computerbaby/index.html (click on "Computer Baby")

This website offers a free printable faces page for your baby.

❦ David Jack

www.davidjack.com/freetape.html

To introduce you to the quality children's music of David Jack, this website offers, free of charge, the children's music CD titled *Dance in Your Pants*. You pay only the shipping and handling. Check out the website for further details.

❦ December Fifth Creations Baby Shower Games

www.dfcreations.com/BabyShower.html

At this website you'll find more than fifty humorous, creative, challenging, and ice-breaking baby shower games! This assortment of free games includes My Water Broke, Pin the Diaper on the Baby, Taste Test Baby Food Game, Mom-to-Be Trivia Game, Guess the Delivery Stats, Diaper Bag Mystery, and more.

❦ Del Monte Nature's Goodness

www.naturesgoodness.com

Nature's Goodness is offering a free lullabies CD ($9.99 retail value) when you send in twelve proofs of purchase (labels or boxtops) from Nature's Goodness baby food products. This ten-song CD features a selection of classic and contemporary music sure to lull your baby to sleep. You can also visit the website for a free sampling of the CD. During your website visit, be sure to sign up for their free mailing list to receive additional valuable offers. This offer is available to residents of the United States only.

Dimetapp (Wyeth Consumer Healthcare)
www.dimetapp.com

Visit Dimetapp's website to receive a free discount coupon for Dimetapp Infant Drops. This offer is available to residents of the United States only.

Ebabyetc.com
www.ebabyetc.com

From time to time, ebabyetc.com offers various baby freebies to their valued customers. Visit their website for details; check back frequently if nothing is available at the present time.

Enfamil
www.efb-mail.com/home.html

The Enfamil website offers free online cards that you can send to a friend or relative. These cute cards contain a section where you can add your own personal message. Themes for these cards include "Pregnancy," "It's a Girl!," "It's a Boy!," "Congratulations," "Birthday," "Thank You," and "Grandparents." Some of these cards are even animated!

Envisage Design Oh Baby!
www.envisagedesign.com/ohbaby

Researchers have found that babies prefer to look at high-contrast images. The Envisage Design website provides free infant stimulation graphics that you can download and print out for your baby to help increase your baby's concentration skills as well as attention span.

❧ First Response
www.1stresponse.com/resourceCorner/freePlanningGuide.asp

Register with First Response to receive a free "Planning a Baby?" brochure, filled with valuable coupons for First Response Ovulation and Pregnancy Test Kits. When you register with them, you will also receive free e-newsletters, special promotions, and more. You can also check out their website for an online ovulation calculator and online due date calculator. This offer is available to residents of the United States only.

❧ The First Years
www.thefirstyears.com (click on "Parents Council")

Expecting parents and parents with children up to the age of three can sign up online to join The First Years "Parents Council." This program, which is free to join, offers several benefits, including the opportunity to test and help develop new products that will help you care for your baby, receive free online childcare tips and newsletters tailored to your child's age, send e-cards to friends and family announcing your child's special first moments, receive a free parenting guide, and more. This offer is available to residents of the United States and Canada.

❧ Fisher-Price
www.fisher-price.com/us/special/offers
www.fisher-price.com/us (Click on "Baby on the Way")

Visit the Fisher-Price website to receive special offers, such as product discounts and contests. During your visit, be sure to sign up to receive the "Pregnancy Playtimes" e-mail newsletter, filled with helpful information about pregnancy and the various stages of pregnancy, fun tidbits and tips for moms, online activities for parents-to-be, and more. This offer is available to residents of the United States and Canada.

❦ Fisher-Price Family

www.fisher-price.com/us/family/form.asp

Residents of the United States can join the Fisher-Price Family mailing list to receive special offers from Fisher-Price, contests, age-appropriate updates for your child, free e-mail newsletters, news on latest products, and more.

❦ Gentle Naturals

www.gentlenaturals.com

Gentle Naturals offers baby products made with pure, natural ingredients, including baby wash, baby cream, and more. Visit the Gentle Naturals website to receive a $2.00 mail-in rebate. This offer is available to residents of the United States only.

❦ Gerber

www.gerber.com/bf/coupon.html

Visit the Gerber website to print out a coupon for $5.00 off the Gerber Premium Feeding System. This offer is available to residents of the United States only.

❦ GoodNites (Kimberly-Clark)

www.goodnites.com/sample

Register online to receive a free printable coupon for money off your next purchase of GoodNites disposable underpants. This offer is available to residents of the United States only.

❦ GrowthSpurts.com

www.growthspurts.com

At GrowthSpurts.com you can create a free website for your child where you can upload your child's photos to share with your family and friends, as well as track your child's growth and development.

❧ Heinz Baby Basics
www.vitalbaby.com/basics/offer.html

Join the Heinz Baby Basics mailing list to receive a free baby spoon from the Heinz Baby Basics line, as well as details on future offers and specials, by filling out the form at the website. This offer is available to residents of Canada only.

❧ Huggies Happy Baby Fun
www.huggies.com/happybabyfun/hppybby.asp

At this cute and creative website you can make and print out a personalized storybook for your child. Children love it when they hear their own name in the story! This website also offers a personalized coloring book for your child to make and print out, plus customized picture frames, a Happy Baby Growth Chart, Create-a-Mobile, songs, games, and more.

❧ Hyland's
www.hylands.com (click on "Consumer Promotions")

Off and on, Hyland's offers promotions and discounts on diaper rash cream, children's medicines, and various other products at the website. If a free promotional offer is not available the first time you visit the website, check back again at a later time.

❧ Invest in Kids
www.investinkids.ca (click on "Join Us")

Invest in Kids is a not-for-profit foundation dedicated to the healthy social, emotional, and intellectual development of children from birth to age five. Visit the website to receive a free Years Before Five Resource Kit, which discusses the importance of early years and highlights the different developmental stages from birth to five years of age, as well as provides activities for each stage of your child's development. This offer is available to residents of Canada only.

✿ iParenting.com

U.S. website: www.iparenting.com/coreg/newsletter.htm
Canadian website: www.iparentingcanada.com

iParenting.com, devoted to the entire family lifecycle from pre-conception through the teenage years, offers more than forty award-winning websites. Parents can sign up at the website to receive a variety of free newsletters, including "Pregnancy Today," "Babies Today," "Breastfeed.com," and many more. When you fill out their online survey, you will also be registered to receive valuable free coupons, special offers, and freebies for you and your child. This offer is available to residents of the United States and Canada.

✿ It's Entirely Personal

www.itsentirelypersonal.com (click on "Request a Footprinting Kit")

Visit the It's Entirely Personal website to register for a free kit that you can use to make a special keepsake of your baby's first footprints. See the website for details. This offer is available to residents of the United States and Canada.

✿ Johnson's Baby

www.johnsonsbaby.com (click on "Promotions")

The Johnson's Baby website offers promotions, sweepstakes, and other free offers from time to time. Visit the website to sign up for their current promotional offers.

❦ Juicy Juice

www.juicyjuice.com/specialoffers

Parents can sign up at the Juicy Juice website to receive Building Blocks of Children's Nutrition, a nutrition guide for infants and toddlers, as well as the Very Best Toddler e-mail newsletter, special offers, promotions, and more. This offer is available to residents of the United States only.

❦ KidKits

www.whatsshowing.on.ca/kids

Free child ID kits are available at this website. If your child goes missing, this printable KidKit will provide police with vital information about your child.

❦ KIDSAFE ID

www.kidsafeid.com

This terrific child safety website allows you to customize, create, and print out your own free KIDSAFE ID Card for your child. Parents can choose from more than thirty colorful, kid-friendly backgrounds, such as baby boy, baby girl, dress-up, baseball, ballet, and music. Visit the website for further details. And while you're there, click on "Do-It-Yourself DNA Kit" to learn how to prepare a home sample of DNA material for your child. All that is required is a cotton swab and two resealable bags. It's really simple to make and worth the effort!

❦ KidsNfeet

www.kidsnshoes.com/kidsnfeet.htm

Visit the KidsNfeet website to print out an easy-to-use shoe measuring system. This printable size ruler will assist you in measuring your children's feet to be sure you get the right fit when shopping for your child's footwear.

❧ Kidz Time

www.kidztime.ca (click on "Kidz Printables")

The Kidz Time website offers lots of free printables for children, including learning activity sheets, flash cards, games, and mazes.

❧ Lampkin Design Group

www.fussybaby.net

This website contains free printable images to help calm or stimulate your baby. You can choose "The Slide Show," which consists of several images that will appear on your computer screen for about ten to fifteen seconds each, or "The Poster," which contains images that you can print out. (Bookmark this site to use during those moments when your child is inconsolable.)

❧ Little Koala

www.littlekoala.com (click on "Postcards")

Little Koala offers free mother and baby and breast-feeding e-mail postcards from Van Gogh, Rembrandt, Monet, and other famous artists. There is also a place where you can write a personalized message below the postcard.

❧ Luvs

www.luvs.com (click on "Register")

Visit the Luvs website to receive announcements, news, and other free offers from Luvs. This offer is available to residents of the United States only.

❧ Mama Bebe & Co.

www.mamabebe.com (click on "Specials and Discounts")

MamaBebe offers a unique selection of adorable baby gifts, such as personalized baby gifts, keepsakes, and baby clothing. Each gift includes a handwritten note card and free gift wrap, and is invoice free. Visit the website to receive 10 percent off your first order of $25 or more. This offer is available to residents of the United States only.

✿ Maternity Mall
www.maternitymall.com (click on "Baby Names")

Maternity Mall offers a free listing of baby names through an interactive search, as well as a free pregnancy tracker and more.

✿ MyADBaby.com
www.myadbaby.com

Visit the website to print out a discount coupon for money off A + D Zinc Oxide Diaper Rash Cream. This offer is available to residents of the United States only.

✿ My Baby Connection
www.mybabyconnection.com

My Baby Connection, a one-stop website for parents of babies and toddlers, offers a huge resource of information and products, organized to help you find what you're looking for quickly. Sign up for their free newsletter, enter their free drawing, or get a free baby website where you can share the joy of your precious baby with your friends and family.

✿ My Gym
www.my-gym.com

My Gym offers fitness programs to help children three months to nine years of age develop physically, cognitively, and emotionally. For a free preview class, visit the website to find the location nearest you, and call for a free preview class in your area.

❧ National Campaign for Hearing Health

www.hearinghealth.net/pages/contact/contact.asp

The National Campaign for Hearing Health focuses on babies and children to make sure that all children have their hearing screened at birth. Visit the website to join the National Campaign for Hearing Health and receive a free infant hearing checklist, a list of hospitals that test newborn hearing, or a free set of earplugs. Be sure to check out the website also for more information on the importance of hearing health. This offer is available to residents of the United States only.

❧ Natrol Nutrition Club

www.natrol.com (click on "Nutrition Club")

Natrol has an extensive line of children's and adults' vitamins, supplements, and formulas. You can join the Natrol Nutrition Club by filling out a brief form at the website. There is no cost to join this club, and as a way of saying thank you for participating, Natrol will send you a Natrol Nutripak, which includes a company brochure, a coupon for the next purchase of any Natrol product, and free sample packets. The Natrol Nutripak is available only to residents of the United States. Residents of Canada who join will benefit from nutrition news and promotional offers.

By joining the Natrol Nutrition Club, you will instantly become eligible to win $100 worth of Natrol products. The contest is open to residents of the United States only. Check out Natrol's website for further contest details.

❧ Nikon

www.coolpix101.com/diaperoffer/splash.html

Sign up online to get a free photo tip diaper bag tag and brochure, courtesy of Nikon and Lamaze. This offer is available to residents of the United States only.

❦ *Parenting*
www.parenting.com/parenting

Moms-to-be can sign up at the *Parenting* website to receive a free Healthy Pregnancy Planner, an online calendar containing personalized weekly pregnancy information. Parents can also visit the website to view photos of weekly fetal development, get access to a baby-namer tool (see below), read numerous parenting articles, and more.

❦ Parenting.com BabyNamer
www.parenting.com/parenting (click on "Pregnancy," then "BabyNamer")

Need help finding a name for your baby? This website offers a free BabyNamer where you can check out the meaning of a baby's name, find the most popular baby names, view baby names from around the world, and more.

❦ Patient Channel
www.clicknineteen.com/babytalk

Visit the website to receive a free copy of *BabyTalk Presents You and Your Baby on the Patient Channel* on DVD or VHS video. There are four television program titles included on this informative video, including "The First Few Days," "The First Few Weeks," "Caring for Your Baby," and "Understanding Their World." This offer is available to residents of the United States only.

❦ Playtex Baby
www.playtexbaby.com/babymagic (click on "Receive Our Newsletter!")

For the latest news about Playtex products, as well as free samples and special offers from Playtex, sign up online for the free PlaytexBaby

.com newsletter. This offer is available to residents of the United States and Canada.

❧ Pregnancy Store

www.pregnancystore.com (click on "Remember?")

The Pregnancy Store offers a full line of pregnancy products, including fertility and ovulation monitors; products for morning sickness relief, pregnancy, and breast-feeding; and great products for your newborn baby. Receive a free downloadable "Remember? What to Bring to the Baby Hospital," a checklist of important items to pack in your hospital bag.

❧ Printable Checklists

www.printablechecklists.com (click on "Parenting")

"When life gets hectic, print out a checklist" is the motto of this parent-friendly website. As things certainly can get hectic when you're having a baby, check out this website for some free printable checklists, including "At the Time of Your Birth Checklist" and "Baby's First Foods Checklist."

❧ Quaker Oatmeal

www.quakeroatmeal.com/toddler/growthchart/offer.cfm

When you sign up at the Quaker Oatmeal website to receive the *Quaker Toddler Newsletter*, you will receive a free growth chart to help you keep track of your child's changing height, as well as a free informational brochure. This growth chart contains a place for your child's name and an area for pictures of your child. This offer is available to residents of the United States and Canada.

❧ Save.ca

www.save.ca

Visit the Save.ca website to sign up for free printable grocery coupons, including coupons for money off Similac Infant Formula, Tide, and more. Consumers can save $5, $10, even $20 on their grocery shopping every week. Simply click on the coupons you want, print them out, and redeem them at grocery stores nationwide. This offer is available to residents of Canada only.

❦ Save.com
www.save.com

The Save.com website offers free printable coupons for groceries and other consumer products, as well as recipes, grocery lists, and more. Visit the website for details. This offer is available to residents of the United States only.

❦ Sesame Street Music Works Video
www.amc-music.org

To help bring music into your children's lives, Sesame Workshop and NAMM-International Music Products Association are offering a free music DVD called *Music Works Wonders*, which stars Hoots, Elmo, and other Muppet characters. To receive your free music DVD, complete a brief online survey. This offer is available to residents of the United States only.

❦ Similasan
www.healthyrelief.com

Similasan products provide relief for the eyes, ears, nose, and throat. Similasan eardrops help relieve earaches in children and are safe for all ages. The website has a downloadable coupon valid for money off any Similasan product.

❦ Simply Kid Stuff
www.simplykidstuff.com/free_stuff.htm

This site offers several free printables, including a printable letter for Santa, a printable Easter Bunny letter, certificates of appreciation, and more!

❧ Snuggle

www.snuggle.com (click on "Special Offers")

Visit the Snuggle website to receive special free offers, enter Snuggle's online sweepstakes, and more. Click on "Snuggle Fun" to send adorable e-cards from the Snuggle bear, or download a Snuggle bear screensaver for your computer.

❧ TLContact.com

www.tlcontact.com

TLContact.com offers a free CarePage service that will save you from making countless phone calls to relay information to concerned relatives and friends when you're expecting a baby or if you have a child who needs to spend time in the hospital. Visit the site for details on setting up your own personalized Web page, uploading photos, and sharing your news. This offer is available to residents of the United States and Canada.

❧ Totally Toddler

www.totallytoddler.com (click on "Save Money Now!")

Totally Toddler is a nursery stain and odor remover and prewash that is used to remove stains and odors caused by food, baby's spit-up, and formula, as well as messes from bed-wetting, grass, and other causes. It is nontoxic and safe to use around children and pets. Visit the website to receive a discount on any Totally Toddler product. This offer is available to residents of the United States only.

❧ Toys "R" Us

www.toysrusemail.com

For a chance to receive valuable offers and special savings from Toys "R" Us, sign up at the website listed above. This offer is available to residents of the United States only.

❦ Triaminic Clinic

www.triaminicclinic.com/promotions.shtml

Visit the Triaminic Clinic website to receive free samples, coupons, and special offers from Triaminic. Parents can also sign up online to receive a free Triaminic Clinic House Call Kit, which includes the following:

- The *Triaminic Clinic Update*, a newsletter that provides useful information, resources, and features on children's health
- The *Triaminic Family Health Organizer* CD-ROM, with important information to help you record and manage your family's health information
- A *Caught by the Cold Catcher* storybook introducing the new super health hero, Cold Catcher
- A sample of new Triaminic Thin Strips with a coupon for money off your first purchase

These offers are available to residents of the United States only.

❦ USA Baby

www.usababy.com/registry/index.html

Complete and submit USA Baby's online form, then print out a coupon that will entitle you to one free teddy bear when you visit a USA Baby store to complete a baby registry. (USA Baby has made this offer available on and off at the website. If the free offer is not currently available, check back again at a later time.) This offer is available to residents of the United States only.

❦ USC Education Savings Plan Inc.

www.resp-usc.com/resp-eng/parents_bib.html

The USC (University Scholarships of Canada) website offers information about saving for your baby's future. Parents can sign up online to receive a free USC kids bib. This offer is available to residents of Canada only.

Free Software Downloads for Parents and Baby

The following websites offer free or try-before-you-buy software for you and your baby that is both fun and educational. The try-before-you-buy downloads are free for a limited time only. If you decide you like the software, you can purchase it after the demo period has expired. In any event, all the software downloads I've listed here are free, with no initial cost to you.

Be sure to test out the BabyType software. It's great for babies who just love to bang away on your computer. My three children loved it!

❧ ABC Color with Me
www.papajan.com/download

ABC Color with Me is a cute software program where kids can color pictures while listening to lively music. Visit the PapaJan.com website to download a free copy of this software for your little one.

❧ ABC Kid Genius
www.zdnet.com/downloads (type "ABC Kid Genius" in the Search box)

ABC Kid Genius is designed to teach toddlers the alphabet, numbers, counting, and reading and spelling using sound, pictures, and video clips. Kids as young as eighteen months can learn to use the keyboard.

❧ Baby Album
www.zdnet.com/downloads (type "Baby Album" in the Search box)

Baby Album software lets you create a multimedia baby album by adding photos, drawings, video, and even audio clips into your Baby Album pages. Record everything that happens during pregnancy, delivery, and the baby's life, and make it available online by creating your child's website.

🦋 BabyCharts

www.zdnet.com/downloads (type "BabyCharts" in the Search box)

The BabyCharts software program allows parents of infants and toddlers to create charts to track their baby's physical development—perfect for parents who want to ensure that nothing is amiss with the physical development of their baby.

🦋 BabyKeys

www.zdnet.com/downloads (type "BabyKeys" in the Search box)

With BabyKeys, your child will have fun pressing the various buttons on the computer keyboard and get entertaining responses with colorful graphics, pictures, music, and audio descriptions of the pictures displayed.

🦋 BabyRecon

www.5star-shareware.com (type "BabyRecon" in the Search box)

BabyRecon is a free statistical analysis tool that allows you to discover the sex of your future child, with a high degree of accuracy. Precision forecasts of 89 to 94 percent have been made. Simply enter the dates of birth for the mother and father and the date of conception, and the program will predict the likelihood of the baby being a boy or a girl.

🦋 BabyStep

www.babystep.com

At this website you can download the free basic version of BabyStep software. This software contains a pregnancy calendar, a baby book, a photo album, an address book, and more.

❧ Baby Ticker

www.babyticker.com

Baby Ticker was developed to keep friends and family informed of your baby's development and new accomplishments. Baby Ticker includes free baby scrapbook website software where you can record all the significant events in your child's life. Friends and family can visit the website to receive updated baby information by viewing the highlights from your baby scrapbook. Visitors will even be able to download and view video clips of the family! Baby Ticker keeps track of the total number of people who have viewed the website and the date and time of their most recent visit. Check out the website for more details.

❧ BabyType

www.raize.com/cproducts/babytype/default.htm

At this website you can download a free ten-day demo version of BabyType software for your baby or toddler, perfect for babies and small children who like to bang away on your computer keyboard. With Baby-Type, you can convert your computer into a child's activity center! When your baby presses a key on the keyboard, BabyType plays a sound on the computer's speakers and displays on the screen a random shape or the letter corresponding to the key that was pressed. The free ten-day demo is fully functional, but to continue playing BabyType after the expiration, you must purchase the software.

❧ BabyWatch

www.babiesonline.com/pregnancy/babywatch/content.asp

BabyWatch is a freeware-shareware program to help you "watch" your pregnancy. It contains thousands of baby names that you can browse through, the meaning of each name, its geographic origin, a personality description that often goes with it, a basic countdown counter, and more. The basic version of BabyWatch is free, but you can order the upgraded version, with additional features, for a fee.

❦ Barnyard Friends

www.5star-shareware.com (type "Barnyard Friends" in the Search box)

Entertain your little one with 123Learn: Barnyard Friends, a free software download featuring assorted farm animals. Your child will enjoy clicking on different things to hear the sounds each animal makes.

❦ CycleWatch

www.zdnet.com/downloads (type "CycleWatch" in the Search box)

The CycleWatch software will help you learn how to track fertility cycles to achieve or avoid pregnancy. CycleWatch records cervical position, displays the ovulation day in your cycle, and more.

❦ Dawn's Due Date Screen Saver

www.dawnsoft.com/dldc.html

Dawn's free Due Date Screen Saver will display your due date and automatically count down the days left until that date. A cute stork picture is displayed with your due date and the days remaining.

❦ Forest Field Trip

www.5star-shareware.com (type "Forest Field Trip" in the Search box)

Your little one can discover all sorts of forest friends with 123Learn: Forest Field Trip, a free software download. She can explore this software by clicking on different things to hear the sounds they make.

❦ Jungle Adventure

www.5star-shareware.com (type "Jungle Adventure" in the Search box)

Your little one can hear all the sounds of the animals in the jungle with 123Learn: Jungle Adventure, a free software download that will take your child on a safari adventure!

❧ MomToBe: The Pregnancy Assistant
www.5star-shareware.com (type "MomToBe" in the Search box)

This computerized pregnancy software enables moms-to-be to monitor the various stages of motherhood. It also provides information on how to prepare for pregnancy aimed at those who are at the "just thinking about getting pregnant" stage. When you are trying to get pregnant, the software provides you with a Basal Body Temperature Chart to indicate when you are ovulating, as well as useful information about how best to get pregnant, the best time to get pregnant, and more. The "You Are Pregnant" section features a Desktop Weekly Calendar to maintain appointments. "Weekly Information" provides a description of the baby, including its possible weight, height, and more. This software will also help you estimate the due date of your baby. Just for fun, the Chinese Sex Calendar helps identify your unborn baby's sex. The trial version of this program is free but has limited monthly baby information. If you enjoy the software, you can purchase the full version.

❧ MyBabyLog
www.zdnet.com/downloads (type "MyBabyLog" in the Search box)

Designed by parents for parents, MyBabyLog tracks your baby's development, including monitoring feeding and sleeping patterns, diaper changes, and more. Print out an activity log for your next doctor's visit.

❧ Right Time Reader
www.zdnet.com/downloads (type "Right Time Reader" in the
    Search box)

This free reading program enables you to teach your infant the printed word in the same way that you already do with the spoken word. This program also contains children's books that you can personalize. You can even create your own children's books with this educational program!

❧ Teletubbies Screensaver
www.freewaresite.com/screensavers/teletubbies.html

Visit this colorful website to download a free, fun, and entertaining Teletubbies screensaver with bright colors, sound effects, and, of course, the Teletubbies!

❧ We-Blocker.com
www.we-blocker.com

We-Blocker is a word-filtering software that will protect you and your family from sexually charged and other inappropriate websites. This free download is available to residents of the United States and Canada.

❧ Who Spilled the Tubby Custard?
www.bbc.co.uk/cbeebies/teletubbies (click on "Fun and Games")

This free software download will take your kids on a fun journey with the Teletubbies and help answer the question, "Who Spilled the Tubby Custard?" Kids will hear a story and learn new words and sounds. Other great features of this site include free Teletubbies e-postcards, games, and fun printables.

Free Film Developing, Prints, and Portrait Offers

I think in my babies' first years of life I must have spent more money on pictures than I did on diapers! When I look back on it now, I'm glad I did. Those pictures are so precious!

If you're anything like me, you're probably going to go out and buy lots of rolls of film, and you'll want to have a couple of professional portraits taken as well.

So go ahead, take tons of pictures, and get your adorable little angel all dolled up for a beautiful portrait sitting, while saving money by checking out some of the free offers listed below.

❦ JCPenney Portraits

In the United States, call 800-59-SMILE

www.jcpenneyportraits.com/freebabystuff

What could be nicer than snuggling your sweet new baby? Nothing really, but free baby stuff is sure a close second. Take advantage of this "Free Stuff" offer to capture special memories of your baby. They grow up before you know it! Receive a free 8 × 10 portrait with no sitting fees ($21.99 value)! Visit the above-listed website for a printable coupon.

This site also shows you how to become a Portrait Club member, providing you with two years of portrait discounts and benefits.

JCPenney Portraits are located in most larger JCPenney stores. Visit their website or call the toll-free number for the location nearest you. This offer is available to residents of the United States only.

❦ Olan Mills

In the United States, call 800-252-6526

www.olanmills.com/indexd.asp

Olan Mills offers eleven free new baby portraits of children three months of age or younger. To register, click on "New Baby?" at the Olan Mills website. Check out the website for other special offers, such as a free birthday club and printable discount coupons.

❦ Picture People Clubs

www.picturepeople.com/club/clubs.html

The Picture People have three different clubs that you can join: Smilestones, the Birthday Club, and the Portrait Club. Smilestones, a club for new moms, offers four free portraits for your baby's first year. When you join the Birthday Club, you will receive a free 8 × 10 portrait and a free Baskin-Robbins ice cream cone (with the purchase of the same). The Portrait Club offers unlimited free sittings for the whole family for one full year, three free portrait sheets, and other special savings for members. The cost to join the Portrait Club is $39.95. Smilestones and the Birthday Club are free to join. Visit the website for more details. This offer is available to residents of the United States only.

❀ PictureTrail
www.picturetrail.com/register/register.cgi

When you sign up for your free online PictureTrail account, you will be able to share your photos online with friends and family, upload photos to as many photo albums as you would like, customize each photo album with graphics and background colors, add MIDI music to your albums, and more. Check out the website for further details. This offer is available to residents of the United States and Canada.

❀ PolaroidPics
www.polaroidpics.com

Receive ten free 4 × 6 prints and e-mails about special offers from Polaroid when you join PolaroidPics. Visit the website for details.

❀ Sears Portrait Studio
In the United States or Canada, call 866-292-4949
www.sears-portrait.com (click on "Coupons")

Log on to the website to receive discount coupons to be redeemed at participating Sears Portrait Studios. Click on "Sign Up" to receive e-mail specials on portrait coupon offers, new contests, and more. This offer is available to residents of the United States and Canada.

❀ Shutterfly
www.shutterfly.com

Shutterfly is a Web-based photo service. When you sign up for a free membership with Shutterfly, you will receive fifteen free 4 × 6 prints and free Shutterfly SmartUpload software as well as free picture storage to help you store and organize all of your pictures online. Visit the website to sign up. This offer is available to residents of the United States and Canada.

❧ Snapfish
www.snapfish.com

When you sign up with Snapfish, you will receive ten free prints the first time you upload to your Snapfish account. Snapfish will also develop your first roll of film free of charge. All you pay is $1.99 for shipping and handling of your prints and negatives. Check out the website for more details. Film processing services are available to residents of the United States only. However, residents of Canada are free to view albums and upload digital pictures.

Free Baby Contests and Sweepstakes

Feeling lucky? Why not enter one of the following contests for a chance to win some terrific prizes, including a year's supply of baby diapers and wipes, gifts, baby products, and more. Good luck!

❧ Babies Today
http://babiestoday.com/photocontest.htm

Babies Today offers a free baby photo contest. This contest is ongoing, and you can send in one photo per weekly contest, entering as many times as you like. Enter your beautiful new baby today!

❧ Baby Bag Online
www.babybag.com (click on "Sweepstakes")

Fill out the online form at the Baby Bag website to win a free gift from one of the Baby Bag vendors. This offer is available to residents of the United States and Canada.

❧ BebeSounds

www.bebesounds.com (click on "Monthly Give-Away")

Visit the BebeSounds website for a chance to win free BebeSounds products when you register for their monthly drawing. This offer is available to residents of the United States only.

❧ Blankees

www.blankees.com/free.htm

Visit the Blankees website to enter their monthly contest to win a free crib-size baby blanket in the style of your choice. This offer is available to residents of the United States and Canada.

❧ GoBabies

www.gobabies.com (click on "Win Free Products")

Enter the GoBabies monthly sweepstakes for a chance to win free baby products. Visit the website for details.

❧ Huggies Super Sweepstakes

www.huggies.com/na/offers/promo/sweepstakes/index.asp

Fill out the online entry form at the Huggies website to win a year's supply of Huggies diapers, baby wipes, and disposable changing pads. Good luck! This offer is available to residents of the United States and Canada.

❧ My Miracle Baby.com, Inc.

In the United States, call 800-342-2509
www.mymiraclebaby.com

My Miracle Baby offers a huge selection of newborn and infant clothing, toys, and personalized gifts at up to 70 percent off retail. Check out the bargain bin for even greater deals. Share your "miracle baby" story or enter your angel in their free baby of the month contest.

❧ Nikon Coolpix 101
www.prideandjoybaby.com

Enter your baby in the Nikon Coolpix Pride and Joy Baby Photo Contest with Best Buy. Your child could win a $25,000 U.S. savings bond for college, and you could win a Nikon Coolpix digital camera family package. Visit the website for details.

❧ Nursery Water Sweepstakes
http://nursery.elwellinc.com/free-stuff.cfm (click on "Special
  Offers")

Visit the website to enter the free Nursery Water Sweepstakes to win a free portrait package for your little one from JCPenney Portraits. Visit the website for details. This offer is available to residents of the United States only.

❧ Pampers
www.pampers.com (click on "Register")

When you register at the Pampers website, not only will you receive free samples and coupons from Pampers, but you will also be automatically entered to win a year's supply of free Pampers products! Visit the website for details. This offer is available to residents of the United States and Canada.

❧ Parents.com
www.parents.com/sweepstakes/sweepstakes.jsp

Parents can sign up to win terrific prizes, trips, and more at the Parents.com website. Click on "Prizes, Products, Promotions" for even more special promotional offers.

Free Stuff from Stores

Many department stores, chain stores, and grocery stores that carry infant wear, maternity wear, and other baby-related merchandise offer free gifts, parenting packs, baby clubs, and discounts to new and expecting parents. Some stores offer discounts for parents of multiples, some will offer free gifts for you and your baby when you register with them, and others give away valuable discount coupons and free samples of brand-name baby products for you to try out.

The best thing that you can do when visiting a store that carries infant wear and other baby-related merchandise is to ask what special offers they have available for new and expecting parents. Keep in mind that many store clerks may feel uncomfortable in pointing out that you are pregnant, especially if you are in the early months, and may hesitate approaching you with their company's offers. Make a point of asking wherever you go to be sure you don't miss out on anything!

The following is a list of stores for you to check out when you're out shopping for your little one.

Drop-In Freebies

If you find any of the following stores in your neighborhood, consider yourself lucky! Drop into any of these stores to receive all kinds of terrific freebies, including free gifts, money-saving coupons, free promotional items for yourself and your baby, as well as the opportunity to sign up for various programs, clubs, and baby registries.

The following is a list of stores for you to check out when you're out shopping for your little one.

❦ Acme Baby Club
www.acmemarkets.com (click on "Save")

For every dollar you spend on baby products at Acme Markets, you will earn one Baby Point. When you collect one hundred Baby Points with your Acme SuperCard, you will receive a $10 gift card. You can apply for a free Acme SuperCard at the courtesy counter at any Acme store location. To receive a free birthday cake when your child's first birthday arrives, bring a copy of his or her birth certificate to a bakery associate at any participating Acme Market. This offer is available only in Acme stores with a bakery department. These offers are available to residents of the United States only.

❦ Babies "R" Us and Toys "R" Us
www.babiesrus.com

When you visit any Babies "R" Us or Toys "R" Us store to register for your baby shower, you will receive free gifts, money-saving coupons, and other free promotional items. You can visit any store location to register, or register at the website. This offer is available to residents of the United States only.

❦ Baby Depot
In the United States, call 888-BCF-COAT
www.coat.com

The Baby Depot has a gift registry for expecting parents. Stop by any store location to register. This offer is available to residents of the United States only.

❦ Eckerd BabyCare Club
In the United States, call 800-325-3737
www.eckerd.com (click on "Baby Care")

Members of the Eckerd BabyCare Club will receive a free membership card in the mail, along with valuable coupons. Members will also receive 10 percent off infant formulas and accessories, children's prescriptions, baby items, the *Talking Babies* newsletter, and more. Visit the website to fill out the online enrollment form to join the free club, or visit a store location to enroll. Call the toll-free number for further details. This offer is available to residents of the United States only.

❦ Meijer
www.meijer.com/babyclub

Expectant parents and anyone with children under the age of three can join the Meijer Baby Club. When you join this free club, you will receive useful information and savings. Meijer also offers a free baby gift registry where you can register for your baby shower with them. Visit a Meijer store location to register, or register online. Check out the website for further details. This offer is available to residents of the United States only.

❦ OshKosh B'Gosh
www.oshkoshbgosh.com

Parents of multiples will receive a special 10 percent discount on their purchase when they visit an OshKosh B'Gosh store location to register for the multiples program. This offer is available to residents of the United States only.

❦ Publix Baby Club
In the United States, call 863-688-7407
www.publix.com/services/clubs

The Publix Baby Club is available to expectant parents and families with children up to twenty-four months. When you join the Publix Baby Club, you will receive coupons for free baby products, a free newsletter, an A–Z baby book published by the American Academy of Pediatrics, and more. Pick up an enrollment form in the baby aisle or at the customer service desk of any Publix Super Market, or call the Publix Baby Club Member Message Line to request more information. This offer is available to residents of the United States only.

✿ Sears

In the United States, call 800-349-4358
In Canada, call 800-211-2111
U.S. website: www.sears.com
Canadian website: www.sears.ca

The following are various free programs offered to new and expecting parents when they visit participating Sears department stores.

• **Sears Request Baby Registry.** When you visit any Sears location to register for your baby shower, you will receive a free gift. You can sign up for your gift registry at the in-store Sears Request kiosk at any Sears location. This offer is available to residents of the United States and Canada.

• **Waiting Game Club.** Drop in at any Sears infants' department, or go online (www.sears.ca) to register for the Waiting Game for expectant mothers who have signed up for the Sears Request Baby Registry, as described in the listing mentioned above. If you are expecting and can correctly guess the due date of your baby, you will receive all of the Sears baby purchases that you have made through your Baby Registry absolutely free! To be eligible for this contest, your birth must be a natural birth, and you must sign up for the contest at least sixty days before your expected due date. Visit any Sears infants' department for details. The Waiting Game is available to residents of Canada only.

• **Sears KidVantage Club.** Drop in at any Sears children's or infants' department for details on the KidVantage Club. This club offers the Wear

Out Warranty. If your infant's or child's clothing or shoes wear out before they're outgrown, Sears will replace the clothing or shoes free in the same size. This offer is available to residents of the United States and Canada. Residents of the United States who join the KidVantage Club will also earn a 15 percent shopping discount off of their next infants' or children's apparel purchase for every $100 (U.S.) that they spend on Sears clothing.

• **Sears Family First Club.** When you sign up (www.sears.ca/e/serv/fam first.htm) for the exclusive Sears Family First Club, you will receive savings on merchandise and services at Sears, including a membership kit containing over $1,000 in savings coupons throughout the year; a one-year subscription to *Today's Parent Magazine*; 250 bonus Sears Club Points on your Sears Card; 10 percent off your first purchase of kids' wear, nursery items, and nursery furniture; and much, much more. The cost to join this club is $24.99. Sign up online, or drop into any Sears kids' wear or toy department to register. This club is available to residents of Canada only.

Toys "R" Us
In Canada, call 800-TOYS-R-US
www.toysrus.com

When you visit any Toys "R" Us store to register for your baby shower in the Babies "R" Us department, you will receive a free parenting starter kit filled with baby essentials, as well as free discount coupons. You will also be added to a mailing list to receive free baby catalogs periodically throughout the year, with additional valuable coupons offering further savings. This offer is available to residents of Canada only.

USA Baby
www.usababy.com

Parents of multiples can drop in at any USA Baby store to receive 10 percent off the sale price of their second duplicate item.

Grocery Store Baby Clubs

Grocery store clubs are popping up everywhere, offering all kinds of programs where you can collect points to save money on baby products and other store merchandise when you shop at these stores. Some of these clubs even offer instant cash-back rewards.

In this section I have listed only some of the grocery stores that offer free new parent or baby clubs. When shopping at your local grocery store, be sure to ask if there is a program available for parents. Many stores do have these clubs available, but you may just not be aware of them.

✿ A&P Baby Bonus Clubs (U.S.)
A&P stores in the United States: A&P, Waldbaum's, SuperFresh, Sav-A-Center, Farmer Jack, Food Basics, and The Food Emporium
www.aptea.com (click on store logo)

Various A&P stores throughout the United States offer a free Baby Bonus Club to their shoppers. As a club member, you will receive $20 instant cash-back every time you spend $200 in baby item purchases using a Bonus Savings Club card. There is no limit to the number of times you can qualify for your $20 cash-back reward. Look for the Baby Bonus Club shelf tags at participating grocery stores to earn free Baby Bonus Points on more than nine hundred items every week. You can apply for a Bonus Savings Club card by filling out an application available on the website that you can print out and bring to the courtesy counter at participating A&P locations, or simply visit a participating A&P location to apply. Many of these stores also have club signs throughout their store that will show you additional savings on numerous other items for club members. When at the checkout counter, simply present your club card to the cashier and the discounts and coupon savings will be automatically deducted from your total bill. This program is available at participating A&P stores only. There may be variations in the Baby Bonus Club program from store to store.

❦ A&P Baby Bonus Clubs (Canada)

A&P stores in Canada: A&P, Dominion, Ultra Food & Drug
In Canada, call 877-76-FRESH
www.freshobsessed.com

The Baby Bonus Club is an exclusive program of A&P, Dominion, and Ultra Food & Drug stores. You can earn Baby Bonus Club Points on more than nine hundred items throughout the store when you present your Air Miles card to the cashier at the front desk. When you accumulate ten points, you will receive a $20 gift certificate. Baby Bonus Club Points are in addition to any regular or bonus Air Miles Reward Miles you earn. To apply, simply go to any participating A&P, Dominion, or Ultra Food & Drug location. Call, or visit the website for further details. There may be variations in the club program from store to store.

❦ Brookshire's—Beginners Baby Club

www.brookshires.com/babyclub/default.aspx

When you sign up for the Brookshire's Beginners Baby Club, you will receive a free welcome gift, free *Beginners* newsletter, free birthday gifts for your child, the latest information on baby care, free valuable baby product coupons, Beginners Bucks, and more. To be eligible to join the Beginners Club, you must first sign up for a free "Thank You Card." Applications are available at the store offices of all Brookshire's stores. Brookshire's Beginners is available to expectant parents and parents with children up to twenty-four months. This program is available to residents of the United States only.

❦ Food Lion

In the United States, call 800-210-9569
www.foodlion.com/TheGoodLife/BabyClub.asp
www.foodlion.com/MyFoodLion/MVPCard.asp

Parents who shop at Food Lion can join the free Baby Steps program to receive free products and money-saving coupons for diapers, baby food, and more. To sign up for the Baby Steps program, simply purchase any brand diapers, size newborn to Stage 4, and use your MVP Card. (To sign up for a free MVP card, fill out the online form and bring it to your nearest Food Lion store, or ask for a form directly at the store office.) They will automatically add your name to their Baby Steps mailing list and you will begin receiving money-saving coupons and offers, like $3 off Pampers Diapers, free Food Lion Brand Isopropyl Alcohol, $1 off Gerber Baby Food, and more!

Continue using your MVP Card and the coupons you receive, and they will continue sending you savings through the mail. You should receive your first Baby Steps approximately four to six weeks after your first diaper purchase. If you do not, please call the number listed above. This offer is available to residents of the United States only.

❧ Price Chopper Baby Club
In the United States, call 800-666-7667 (Option 1)
www2.pricechopper.com/babyclub

When you join Price Chopper's free Baby Club, you will receive free rewards and savings. Other member benefits include a free birthday cake for your child's first birthday, free baby newsletters tailored to your child's age, free money-saving coupons, plus automatic entry into their monthly sweepstakes. Visit your nearest store location to sign up, or fill out the online form at the website. Be sure to include your child's birth date or expected birth date so they can send you age-appropriate coupons. This offer is available to residents of Pennsylvania, New York, Connecticut, Massachusetts, Vermont, and New Hampshire.

❧ ShopRite Baby Bucks
www.shoprite.com/babybucks/intro.htm

When you sign up for the ShopRite Baby Bucks program, you will automatically get $5 off your next shopping order of $50 or more on baby items at any ShopRite location. Visit any ShopRite store location to register, or register online. This offer is available to residents of the United States only.

❀ Smith's Baby Fresh Reward Points Program
In the United States, call 800-764-8897
www.smithsfoodanddrug.com/freshvalues/babyclub_details.htm

For every dollar you spend on baby items (including diapers and formula) at Smith's Food & Drug Stores, you will earn one point when you use your Fresh Values card. When you sign up for a Fresh Values card, you will save $10 on your groceries every time you accumulate two hundred Baby Fresh Reward points. You will also receive fifty free Baby Fresh Reward points when you sign up for the Smith's Baby Fresh Rewards Program. As a member of the Baby Fresh Rewards Program, you will also be entitled to receive a free can of powdered infant formula for every eight cans that you buy, a free birthday cake to help you celebrate your little one's first birthday, special manufacturers' coupons, and other offers and discounts—even free cookies from the bakeshop for your child! Visit your local Smith's Food & Drug Store to register, or call for further details. This offer is available to residents of the United States only.

❀ Weis Markets Baby Care Club
www.weis.com (click on "Baby Care")

When you sign up for the Weis Markets Baby Care Club, you can earn free baby products, including baby food, changing products, diapers, nursing products, and more. To join, simply sign up for the Weis Rewards Club and they will keep track of all of your baby purchases. They will automatically send your reward certificate once you qualify. This offer is available to residents of the United States only.

Free Parenting Books, Magazines, and Other Literature

Shortly after you give birth, the nurse at the hospital hands you your beautiful bundle of joy, all wrapped up in a blanket and smelling sweet and new after his very first bath. A soft smile crosses your face as you exchange loving glances with your husband. Next, your eyes slowly move back down to your beautiful new baby once again. Ahhh . . . what an angel! But suddenly you realize, as you glance around the hospital room in a panic, that you've been left alone with this darling little infant. Your husband jumps up. "What, no instructions?!" you hear him yell, as he desperately runs up and down the halls to find the nearest available nurse.

I bought a new TV last week, and it came with instructions. My new VCR came with instructions. Even an electric can opener comes with instructions. Help!

I think all new parents feel a certain amount of anxiety or even panic after their baby is first born: "What if I do something wrong?" "What do I do when the baby starts to cry?" "What if I can't remember how to change a diaper?" Don't worry. These feelings are completely natural.

As a new parent, you want to do what is best for your baby. The terrific parenting books, magazines, and literature that I have listed in this chapter are available to educate you in all areas of your pregnancy, childbirth, and the care of your baby, as well as to help give you the confidence you need to be the best parent you can be.

When in doubt, keep in mind the wise words of the late Dr. Spock, a beloved father, author, and pediatrician who influenced millions of parents around the world: "Trust yourself. You know more than you think you do."

Parenting Books

The following free books are exceptional—must-haves for all new parents and parents-to-be! They cover pregnancy, childbirth, child care, health and nutrition, and many other important topics of parenting.

❧ Family Communications Inc.
In Canada, call 416-537-2604 (sorry, not a toll-free number)

Call to receive a free 178-page reference book titled *The New Quick Reference Baby and Child Care Encyclopaedia*, rated by four hundred Canadian doctors to be the best single source of child care information. This book is a special gift from the publishers of *Best Wishes* magazine and is free for a limited time only. This offer is available to residents of Canada only.

❧ State Farm Insurance
In the United States or Canada, call 888-733-8368

Call to receive *Mayo Clinic Complete Book of Pregnancy and Baby's First Year* for free. This comprehensive 712-page hardcover book guides you through each phase of pregnancy, birth, and baby's exciting and important first year. This offer is available to residents of the United States and Canada.

Parenting Magazines

There are a lot of great parenting magazines on the market today, with so much terrific parenting information and advice. I actually subscribed to three of them when I was expecting and devoured every page. The articles were always up-to-date and provided tons of entertainment, information, and resources for new or expecting parents.

Following are some of the top parenting magazines on the market today, including *Parents, Parenting, Today's Parent, American Baby*, and *Baby Talk*. Many of these magazine offers are absolutely free. And for others, you can receive a free trial issue to give you a chance to decide if you would like to subscribe further. Your first issue is always free, and you can cancel any further issues, if you wish. So if you're not sure which parenting magazine you would like to subscribe to, here's a great chance to try them out for free!

American Baby

In the United States, call 800-678-1208
www.americanbaby.com (click on "Free Offers")

For some sixty-five years, *American Baby* magazine has been the most trusted source of information for new or expectant parents. It features helpful articles on every area of parenting, including health, development, and nutrition. Every issue offers money-saving coupons for brand-name baby products. For a free subscription to *American Baby* magazine, sign up online at the website listed above. Residents of the United States can also sign up by calling the toll-free number. This offer is available to residents of the United States and Canada.

Baby Talk

In the United States, call 800-395-1976
www.parenting.com/parenting/magazines/babytalk.html

Baby Talk is America's number one magazine for your baby's first year of life. It contains information for new or expectant parents. Your subscription for ten issues is absolutely free, no strings attached. Call or register online to begin your free subscription. This offer is available to residents of the United States only.

❦ *Connecting@Home* **Magazine for Moms**
www.freemagazineformoms.com

The *Connecting@Home* magazine contains recipes, tips, hobbies, home décor, health and fitness, family and frugal ideas, as well as help for working at home. Visit the website to sign up for a free copy. This offer is available to residents of the United States only.

❦ **March of Dimes**
mama.modimes.org (click on "Free Materials")

The March of Dimes offers *Mama: Your Guide to a Healthy Pregnancy* free of charge. This is an award-winning magazine for pregnant women and new moms. It contains practical and fun information for parents-to-be, including articles on pregnancy planning, nutrition, growth and development, and more. Sign up for a free copy at the website. This offer is available to residents of the United States and Canada.

❦ *MOMSense* **Magazine**
www.gospelcom.net/mops (click on "Mom Resources")

MOMSense magazine provides practical information and inspiration, especially for mothers of preschoolers. Sign up online to request a free copy and free *MOMSense* e-mail. This offer is available to residents of the United States and Canada.

❦ *Parenting*
www.parenting.com/parenting

Parenting magazine offers tons of parenting articles; information on newborn care, nutrition, and outdoor activities; delicious recipes; health and safety tips; and more. Log on to this website to get a free preview issue of *Parenting* magazine. This offer is available to residents of the United States and Canada. You can also click on "Free Magazines" at the website to get a free subscription offer from *Baby Talk* magazine (United States only). Click on "Free Newsletters" to sign up for free pregnancy and baby newsletters.

❀ *Parents*

In the United States, call 800-727-3682
www.parents.com (click on "Risk-Free Magazines")

Parents magazine delivers reliable child care advice and helps to make raising your baby easier, more fun, and more rewarding. Residents of the United States and Canada can register online to receive a free trial issue of *Parents* magazine. Residents of the United States can also call to order as well.

❀ *Parents Canada*

www.parentscanada.com

Parents Canada magazine contains loads of parenting information, including pregnancy, labor and birth, and more. Sign up online for a free subscription. This offer is available to residents of Canada only.

❀ *S-Magazine*

U.S. website: www.s-mag.com (click on "Register Now")
Canadian website: www.s-mag.ca

Procter & Gamble's *S-Magazine* is an electronic magazine geared toward parents to help simplify their lives, based on value-added content, tips, tools, and brand-specific solutions. A popular section of the magazine is the "Offer Corner" where consumers can sign up to receive advertised offers from Procter & Gamble and other companies. For a free subscription to *S-Magazine*, click on "Register Now."

✿ Taking Good Care

In the United States, call 877-244-5332

Call to sign up for the Sesame Street Goes to the Doctor Program, funded by Pfizer, from the Children's Television Workshop. When you sign up for this program, you will receive a special edition of *Sesame Street Parent's Magazine* titled *Taking Good Care*, which includes a bright Elmo poster. This magazine explains how antibiotics should be used wisely, how to help children with common illnesses, how to alleviate fear when children go to the doctor, and other health-related information. This offer is available to residents of the United States only.

✿ Today's Parent

In Canada, call 800-567-8697
www.todaysparent.com

Today's Parent magazine is a Canadian magazine for parents of children from birth to twelve years of age. The magazine offers informative articles on parenting issues, health and safety concerns, lifestyle, and food and nutrition, as well as information on child development and behavior. Call or log on to the *Today's Parent* website for information about how you can receive a free issue.

Today's Parent offers two additional free magazines to parents who are expecting: *Pregnancy and Birth* and *Newborn*. These excellent prenatal and postnatal publications are available free of charge at most doctors' offices. Ask for a free copy at your next prenatal or postnatal visit. These offers are available to residents of Canada only.

✿ Twins

In the United States or Canada, call 888-55-TWINS
www.twinsmagazine.com

Published by The Business Word Inc., *Twins* magazine is dedicated to making life more enjoyable and easier for parents of multiples. The magazine contains birth stories, tips on raising multiples, and more.

Call to receive a risk-free trial issue of *Twins: The Magazine for Parents of Multiples,* or download a free issue from the website. This offer is available to residents of the United States and Canada.

❦ *Vegetarian Baby & Child*
www.vegetarianbaby.com

The Vegetarian Baby website offers tons of free vegetarian recipes, including delicious vegetarian recipes for baby and the whole family. Visit the website to sign up for their free *Vegetarian Baby & Child Online Magazine.* When you sign up for their free semimonthly newsletter, *Vegetarian Baby & Child Email Newsletter*, you will also have a chance to receive a free gift valued at $25. Visit the website for details.

Other Parenting Literature

The educational pamphlets and brochures discussed in the following section cover many parenting topics, including child safety, breast-feeding tips and advice, postpartum depression, medical concerns, nutrition, and your baby's development—and of course, they're free!

❦ Child Care Aware
1319 F Street NW
Suite 500
Washington, DC 20004-1106
In the United States or Canada, call 800-424-2246
www.childcareaware.org (click on "Publications")

Child Care Aware is committed to helping families find the highest quality child care and child care resources in their community. Families can call or go online to be directly connected to the Child Care Resource and Referral agency within their own community.

The following free parenting publications are available online or by calling the number listed above.

• *All in the Family—Making Child Care Provided by Relatives Work for Your Family.* If you are planning on using relatives to care for your child while you work or go to school, read this brochure to help make this a good choice for you, your child, and the relative caring for your child.

• *Child Care Resource and Referral in Your Local Community.* Child Care Resource and Referral services are available in most local communities, providing many valuable services to families. This tip sheet describes what your local Child Care Resource and Referral program can do for you.

• *Choosing Quality Child Care for a Child with Special Needs.* There are important factors to consider when choosing quality child care for a child with special needs. This brochure provides parents with information to help them choose quality child care for their special needs child.

• *Five Steps to Choosing Safe and Healthy Child Care.* When choosing child care for your child, you want to be sure to select a setting that is both safe and healthy. This brochure provides guidelines for families in choosing safe and healthy child care in various settings.

• *Five Steps to Choosing Summer Child Care.* This brochure provides parents with guidelines for choosing a quality summer care program for their child.

• *Give Your Child Something That Will Last a Lifetime . . . Quality Child Care!* This brochure provides parents with helpful steps to choosing quality child care, as well as a checklist to use when choosing a child care home or center.

• *Making the Transition from Child Care to Kindergarten: Working Together for Kindergarten Success.* This guide offers information and guidance on how you can make sure that your children are involved in activities that will prepare them for kindergarten.

• *Learning to Read & Write Begins at Birth.* This brochure will help explain how you and your child's caregiver can best build your child's early reading and writing skills.

• *Finding Help Paying for Child Care.* This informative brochure will help you learn how you might be able to reduce your child care costs by taking advantage of child care subsidies and tax credits and exploring alternatives to full-time care.

• *A Guide for Dads: Give Your Child an Early Lead in Life . . . Quality Child Care.* Fathers who get involved with their children's care and education make a real difference in their children's success in school and life. This brochure was written to help fathers learn how to get and stay involved with their child's early care and education, as well as provide tips for choosing the right child care for their child.

• *Matching Your Infant's or Toddler's Style to the Right Child Care Setting.* This brochure offers information on how to use what you know about your infant or toddler, such as personal style and activity level, to help you select a child care setting that's just right for your child.

❦ Depression After Delivery, Inc.

www.depressionafterdelivery.com (click on "Download Brochure")

Depression After Delivery provides support for women with ante- and postpartum depression. Visit the website for further information on this topic, as well as to download a free brochure. This offer is available to residents of the United States and Canada.

❦ Dorel Juvenile Group

www.coscoinc.com/services/brochures/brochures.html

Go online to download a free *Travel with Baby* brochure targeting car safety, as well as the *Travel Time* brochure, which contains information regarding strollers and how to select the stroller that is perfect for your needs.

❦ FamilyCare

www.familycareproducts.com/guidebook.asp

Log on to this website to receive the free Recovery Zone guidebook *Mommy, I Don't Feel Good*. This guidebook will teach you how to set up a comfortable place in your home to nurture your child back to health when she isn't feeling well. This offer is available to residents of the United States only.

❦ Ferring Inc.

In Canada, call 800-970-4224
www.bedwetting.ferring.ca

Ferring offers practical solutions to help with your child's bed-wetting problem. Call for free information about bed-wetting or to talk to a registered nurse. Residents of Canada can call the information line 24/7.

❦ Growing Child, Inc.

www.growingchild.com

Growing Child, a monthly child development newsletter, is timed to the monthly age of your child. This newsletter is available to parents of children age six or younger. You can download a free sample issue of *Growing Child*. This offer is available to residents of the United States and Canada.

❦ GuideYourChildren

www.guideyourchildren.com

This excellent parenting site is offering a free *Stressless Parenting Report* and *SuperFoods Report*, as well as a parenting manual that you can download instantly, which guarantees to improve and solve any parenting problems and simplify your life.

❦ Juvenile Products Manufacturers Association

JPMA Public Information
15000 Commerce Parkway

Suite C

Mt. Laurel, NJ 08054

www.jpma.org (type "Safe and Sound for Baby" in the Search box)

The free sixteen-page brochure *Safe & Sound for Baby* illustrates the proper use of many juvenile products, including car seats, changing tables, cribs, crib toys, pacifiers, infant bedding, carriers and swings, carriages and strollers, high chairs, gates and enclosures, infant seats, and more. The brochure also provides safety information on bathing and feeding, household dangers, electrocution, suffocation, and strangulation. For a free copy of this brochure, send a self-addressed, stamped business-size envelope to Juvenile Products Manufacturers Association. Be sure to affix the proper U.S. postage. A downloadable version of this brochure can be found at the website. This offer is available to residents of the United States and Canada.

❦ Keep Kids Healthy

www.keepkidshealthy.com/breast-feeding/guide

KeepKidsHealthy.com is an excellent medical and parenting website. Visit the website to download a free breast-feeding guide with information on how to tell if your baby is getting enough milk, breast-feeding problems, sore nipples, and more.

❦ March of Dimes

1275 Mamaroneck Avenue

White Plains, NY 10605

In the United States or Canada, call 888-663-4637

www.marchofdimes.com/aboutus/request_form.asp

Call or visit their website to obtain the following materials:

• *Are You Ready? A Guide to Planning a Healthy, Happy Pregnancy*. This booklet helps parents-to-be ask and answer tough questions: Are you ready physically to have a baby? Are you ready emotionally? Are you ready financially? This booklet will also help you calculate your due date and give you advice on what to do once you're pregnant, as well as list some things that dads can do during your pregnancy. It also includes advice on getting pregnant, choosing a health care provider, and breaking unhealthy habits. In addition, it features a worksheet for keeping track of important information, such as dates and phone numbers.

• *Genetic Counseling*. This twelve-page booklet shows how family histories and testing can predict many birth defects. It answers questions about genetics and inherited traits, genes, and chromosomes and provides information about testing genetic conditions. It also explains how genetic counseling can help. A family tree is included.

❦ Playtex Baby Magic
In the United States, call 888-532-2229

Call for a free Playtex Baby Magic brochure on caring for your baby's skin. This offer is available to residents of the United States only.

❦ PregnancyWeekly.com
www.pregnancyweekly.com

Sign up for a free electronic newsletter that will support you through a happy, healthy pregnancy.

❦ Safe Kids Canada
180 Dundas Street West
Suite 2105
Toronto, ON M5G 1Z8
In Canada, call 888-SAFETIPS
www.safekidscanada.ca

According to Safe Kids Canada, injuries are the number one cause of death and disability among Canadian children. Safe Kids Canada is a national charity dedicated to providing parents and children with the information they need to reduce the number of injuries to children across Canada. Call or write to receive free professional literature on childhood injury prevention. This offer is available to residents of Canada only.

❧ SeatBelt.com
www.seatbelt.com/safety-page1.html

Visit the website to view the *What to Expect Guide to Car Seat Safety* booklet, which offers information on choosing the right type of car seat, on when to switch to a front-facing seat, and on how long a child should be in a booster seat, along with other car seat safety information. This offer is available to residents of the United States and Canada.

❧ Sharn, Inc.
In the United States or Canada, call 800-325-3671
www.sharn.com

Call for the free brochure *Tips About Giving Your Baby Medicine*. This offer is available to residents of the United States and Canada.

❧ Tiny Love
In the United States or Canada, call 888-TINY-LOVE
www.tinylove.com (click on "Free Developmental Booklet")

Tiny Love manufactures soft developmental toys made of high-quality material. Call or visit the website to request a free catalog and *Your Baby's Development Guide*, a colorful booklet containing useful information about child development from birth to twenty-four months. The booklet is arranged by age and developmental element.

Tiny Love also has a "buy 1, get 1 free" program for parents of twins, triplets, quadruplets, or more on the first order placed with Tiny Love. Ask for details.

These offers are available to residents of the United States and Canada.

❧ Underwriters Laboratories

In the United States, call 877-UL-4-SAFE

Call for a free room-by-room home safety checklist and other home safety tips. This offer is available to residents of the United States only.

❧ Viacord

In the United States, call 866-565-2221
In Canada, call 866-668-4895
www.viacord.com

Umbilical cord blood may be a component of future therapy for your baby or an immediate family member as it is rich in stem cells, which can be used in the treatment of many different cancers, genetic diseases, blood disorders, and immune deficiencies. Thanks to medical advances, your newborn's cord blood can be preserved at delivery to potentially treat more than forty-five life-threatening diseases where an umbilical cord blood stem cell transplant may be appropriate. Call today for your free cord blood information kit. This offer is available to residents of the United States and Canada.

❧ Zero to Three

In the United States, call 877-565-5465
www.zerotothree.org/magic/main.html

The Magic of Everyday Moments Campaign, developed in partnership by Zero to Three and the Johnson & Johnson Pediatric Institute, focuses on how parents can build their baby's social, emotional, and intellectual development through interaction during everyday moments and daily activities such as feeding, bathing, and grocery shopping. The Magic of Everyday Moments booklets show parents how everyday activities can be meaningful opportunities to connect with their children. You can download the set of five booklets at no charge. Or you can call to order hard copies of these booklets, but there is a shipping and handling fee of $6 (U.S.) for all five booklets.

Following are the five booklets offered:

• *The Magic of Everyday Moments (0–4 Months)*. This booklet discusses the things that your baby needs most, how to read your baby's cues, comforting your newborn, what it's like for you as a parent at this stage, and more.

• *The Magic of Everyday Moments (4–6 Months)*. Topics addressed here include what mom and dad might be experiencing during this period, feeding your baby, playing with your baby, reading your baby's cues, and more.

• *The Magic of Everyday Moments (6–9 Months)*. This booklet focuses on what mom and dad might be experiencing through this period, bath time, saying good night, what your baby needs most at this age, and more.

• *The Magic of Everyday Moments (9–12 Months)*. Topics discussed in this booklet include hellos and goodbyes, grocery shopping, reading your baby's cues, what it's like for you as the parent at this stage, and more.

• *The Magic of Everyday Moments (12–15 Months)*. This booklet discusses what it's like for mom and dad during this toddler period, taking a walk, reading to your baby, and more.

Free Maternity, Baby Wear, and Baby Product Catalogs

Being a busy parent, you might not always have the time to head out to the mall to make purchases for your baby.

When things get really busy and you'd rather stay home than face hordes of shoppers at the mall, consider ordering from a catalog. It can be a simple and convenient way to shop, definitely saving you time and often money, as many of these catalog companies don't have all the overhead costs of running an actual store and can afford to list their prices lower than competitors' prices.

The following companies offer free catalogs that carry tons of products for you or your baby, including a great assortment of adorable baby outfits, practical nursing wear, baby and nursery accessories, and more.

Avent America, Inc.
In the United States or Canada, call 800-54-AVENT
www.aventamerica.com

Call Avent for a free brochure featuring bottle and breast-feeding products. This offer is available to residents of the United States and Canada.

❧ **BabyBecause**

In the United States, call 866-734-2634

www.babybecause.com

BabyBecause (formerly Organic Bébé) offers tons of natural products for babies, children, and mothers, such as Baby's Only Organic Formula, Earth's Best Organic Baby Food, organic bedding and clothing, natural skin care items, and cloth diapers. Call or go online for a free catalog of products. This offer is available to residents of the United States only.

❧ **Baby BumbleBee**

In the United States or Canada, call 888-984-5500

www.babybumblebee.com/v2/pages/receive_mail.cfm

Baby BumbleBee provides parents with educationally appropriate materials for infants and toddlers, including educational videos and more. You can order a free catalog by calling or by filling out the online request form. This offer is available to residents of the United States and Canada.

❧ **Baby Catalog of America**

In the United States, call 800-PLAYPEN

www.babycatalog.com

Guaranteeing the lowest advertised prices, the Baby Catalog of America offers everything you'll need for your baby from birth through the toddler stage, such as name-brand monitors, toys, books, strollers, car seats, crib and twin bedding, and nursery décor. You'll get discounts from 10 to 50 percent off pregnancy, baby, and toddler products, regardless of whether you shop online or over the phone. Residents of the United States can call to order a free printed catalog. Residents of the United States and Canada can view the entire catalog online.

This company also has a baby shower and gift registry. Shower guests can buy online and view what has been previously purchased. Check out the website for details.

For a $25 (U.S.) fee, customers can sign up to join the Baby Club to save an additional 10 percent on most purchases. Again, check out the website for details.

This company has an outlet store in West Haven, Connecticut, which carries everything from the website plus more!

❦ Baby Einstein
www.babyeinstein.com (click on "About Us," then "Request a
  Brochure")

Baby Einstein offers a wide assortment of interactive developmental products for babies, such as DVDs, videos, music CDs, books, and toys.

For a free Baby Einstein product brochure, visit the website. This offer is available to residents of the United States and Canada.

❦ Baby Holder
In the United States, call 800-637-9426
In Canada, call 949-361-1089 (sorry, not a toll-free number)
www.babyholder.com

Call for a free catalog of nursing clothes, bras, nighties, breast pumps, and more. A free instructional video is included.

❦ Babystyle
In the United States, call 877-ESTYLES
www.babystyle.com

Call or visit the website to order a free Babystyle catalog featuring the latest in maternity fashions plus toys, gifts, clothing, and other essentials for your baby. This offer is available to residents of the United States only.

Babystyle also offers a convenient baby registry with an automatic "Thank-You" list that keeps track of who gave you what and when. Check out the website for details.

❦ Born to Love

> In the United States or Canada, call 905-725-2559 (sorry, not a toll-free number)
>
> www.borntolove.com (click on "Catalogue")

At Born to Love, you will find everything you need for your newborn. There is a large assortment of diapers and diapering accessories, as well as tons of sewing patterns that you can order, such as sewing patterns for a baby's layette, toy patterns, patterns to make your own car seat cover, hat and mitten patterns, and infant clothing patterns. Residents of the United States and Canada can view the catalog online or order a free catalog by calling.

Born to Love also offers a Catalogue Request Center at www.borntolove.com/catalogues.html. Here you can request an assortment of catalogs from different companies to be forwarded to you free of charge. Among the other companies whose catalogs you can choose from are Babyworks, Miracle Baby, and Natural Baby. This offer is available to residents of the United States and Canada.

❦ Combi International

> www.combi-intl.com/combi/catalog.htm

To receive a free catalog from Combi with a listing of baby products, including strollers, high chairs, and other baby accessories, fill out the form at the website. Catalogs are available to residents of the United States only.

❦ Ecobaby Organics

> In the United States or Canada, call 888-326-2229
>
> www.ecobaby.com (click on "Free Catalog")

To receive a free color catalog filled with information on breast-feeding clothing and supplies, cotton and wool organic baby clothing and bedding, wooden toys and furniture, a large assortment of diapers, and educational infant aids, call or log on to the Ecobaby website.

Ecobaby also has a baby shower registry where you can send in the names and addresses of thirty of your guests, together with your request list, and Ecobaby will send a catalog to each guest with your special requests. This offer is available to residents of the United States and Canada.

❧ Elizabeth Lee Designs

In the United States, call 800-449-3350

www.elizabethlee.com

Elizabeth Lee offers a large assortment of sewing patterns, such as patterns for your baby's nursery décor, diaper bag patterns, infant dress patterns, sweet little layette patterns, and car seat and stroller cover patterns. Also available is a great selection of patterns designed for the breast-feeding mom. Call for a free catalog. This offer is available to residents of the United States only.

❧ Fuzzi Bunz

In the United States or Canada, call 866-DRY-BABY

www.fuzzibunz.com

Fuzzi Bunz are rash-free, leak-free, waterproof cloth diapers by Mother of Eden. Call to request a free catalog of their diapering products. This offer is available to residents of the United States and Canada.

❧ Graham Kracker

In the United States, call 800-489-2820

www.grahamkracker.com (click on "Order Catalog")

Call for a free catalog of custom bedding for baby and child. This offer is available to residents of the United States only.

❧ Heart Thoughts

In the United States, call 800-524-2229

www.heart-thoughts.com

Call to receive free birth announcement samples and a catalog. This offer is available to residents of the United States only.

❦ JCPenney

In the United States or Canada, call 800-JCP-GIFT

www.jcpenney.com/jcp/default.asp (click on "Catalogs," then "Maternity Collection" or "The Baby Book")

JCPenney's Maternity Collection catalog features maternity fashions for all seasons and occasions. JCPenney's Baby Book offers a selection of nursery furniture, car seats, strollers, and more. Call or visit the website to request a free catalog. This offer is available to residents of the United States and Canada.

❦ Jocus Educational Toys

In Canada, call 800-361-4587 (ext. 9351)

Jocus, a Canadian company established in 1978, offers wonderful, affordable toys, games, puzzles, and crafts for every stage of child development, as well as an extensive line of role-play costumes and multicultural puppets and dolls. They are the exclusive distributor of the Veritech independent math and language program for ages three to twelve. To receive a free catalog, earn free toys as a hostess, or find out how to become a Jocus representative, call the toll-free number listed, or send an e-mail to Kerkhof@ezlink.ca for more information. This offer is available to residents of Canada only.

❦ Kidalog

In the United States or Canada, call 780-672-1763 (sorry, not a toll-free number)

www.kidalog.com (click on "Request a Catalogue")

Kidalog (formerly Baby Love Products) offers thousands of baby, child, and mother care products. Call or visit the website to request a free catalog. This offer is available to residents of the United States and Canada.

❧ Lands' End Inc.

In the United States or Canada, call 800-356-4444

www.landsend.com (click on "Kids'," then "Latest Kids' Catalog")

Lands' End offers an assortment of adorable baby outfits, diaper bags, swimwear, bedding, blankets, and more. To receive the latest kids' catalog, call or request one online. This offer is available to residents of the United States and Canada.

❧ Little Me

In the United States, call 800-533-5437

Call to receive a free baby wear brochure of adorable swimsuits and dresses, sleepwear and playwear for newborns and infants, preemie clothing, gift sets, bath sets, and more. This offer is available to residents of the United States only.

❧ Little Tikes

In the United States or Canada, call 888-832-3203

www.littletikes.com (click on "Consumer Service")

Call to receive a free color catalog showcasing some of the newest "toys that last" from Little Tikes. You can also request a catalog at the website. This offer is available to residents of the United States and Canada.

❧ Liz Lange Maternity

In the United States or Canada, call 888-616-5777

www.lizlange.com (click on "Request a Catalog")

For a free catalog of the latest maternity fashions from Liz Lange, visit their website or call the toll-free number listed above. This offer is available to residents of the United States and Canada.

❧ Mia Bambini and Company
www.miabambini.com

This cute website offers an assortment of baby clothing, including dresses and skirts, swimwear, tops, bottoms, footwear, and diaper products. Click on "Register Now" to receive the latest catalog via e-mail. This offer is available to residents of the United States and Canada.

❧ Motherhood Maternity
In the United States or Canada, call 800-4MOM2BE
www.motherhood.com

Call to receive a free maternity product catalog. This offer is available to residents of the United States and Canada.

❧ Motherwear
In the United States, call 800-950-2500
www.motherwear.com

Call or visit the website to request a free copy of Motherwear's color catalog featuring a full line of nursing clothing, nursing bras, breast-feeding products, pumps, accessories, and more. This catalog also contains a detailed sizing guide to help you select a nursing bra in the right size. The Motherwear website presents current and up-to-date breast-feeding information, as well as a breast-feeding booklet titled *Essential Breastfeeding Guide*, which you can download. This offer is available to residents of the United States only.

❧ Mustela
In the United States, call 800-422-2987
www.mustelausa.com

Mustela has been taking care of babies since 1950. They offer hypoallergenic products, formulated for the delicate skin of newborns, as well as maternity skin-care products for expectant mothers. Call to receive a free product brochure, or visit the website to sign up for Mustela's free newsletter or to enter their online sweepstakes. This offer is available to residents of the United States only.

Natural Baby

www.store.yahoo.com/naturalbaby/index.htm (click on "Catalog Request")

Each of the items at Natural Baby is environmentally safe, organic, and natural. Natural Baby offers an assortment of baby items, including blankets and bedding, toys, clothing, and diapers, as well as herbal medicines, homeopathic remedies, and skin care products. Visit the Natural Baby website to request a free catalog. This offer is available to residents of the United States only.

One Step Ahead

In the United States or Canada, call 800-274-8440
www.onestepahead.com (click on "Request a Catalog")

Call to receive a free catalog offering a great selection of baby products, including strollers, carriers, car seats, and more. You can also request a catalog online. This offer is available to residents of the United States and Canada.

Peg-Pérego

In the United States, call 800-671-1701
In Canada, call 800-953-4488
www.perego.com

The Peg-Pérego catalog offers a great assortment of infant car seats, high chairs, strollers, ride-on vehicles, and more. Call, or visit the website to receive a free catalog and list of dealers. This offer is available to residents of the United States and Canada.

❦ **Perfectly Safe**

> www.kidsstuff.com (click on "Perfectly Safe," then "Request
>   Catalog")

Dedicated to child safety, the Perfectly Safe catalog offers child-proofing products for the entire home, your car, and travel. To receive a free catalog, visit the website. This offer is available to residents of the United States only.

❦ **Playstore**

> In the United States, call 877-876-1111
> www.playstoretoys.com

Call for a free product catalog featuring quality wooden and natural toys, dress-up costumes, music and art supplies, games, dolls and puppets, playhouses, and more. This offer is available to residents of the United States only.

❦ **Pride and Joy Announcements**

> In the United States or Canada, call 800-574-9227
> www.newbabyannouncements.com

Pride and Joy offers custom printed birth announcements and thank-you cards. Call to request a free Pride and Joy birth announcement catalog and samples. This offer is available to residents of the United States and Canada.

❦ **Right Start**

> In the United States or Canada, call 800-Little1
> www.rightstart.com

The Right Start catalog offers products for mothers, infants, and children, including furniture, developmental toys, books, safety devices, music, videos, high chairs, and strollers. Call to order a free catalog. You can also register for the Right Start's baby registry online or by visiting a Right Start store location. This offer is available to residents of the United States and Canada.

❦ Safe Beginnings

In the United States or Canada, call 800-598-8911
www.safebeginnings.com (click on "Request Our Catalog")

Call or visit the website to request a free catalog of safety products and infant or toddler accessories.

❦ Stork Avenue

In the United States, call 800-861-5437
www.storkavenue.com (click on "Catalog Request")

Stork Avenue is one of the nation's premier Internet and catalog providers of birth announcements and invitations. Residents of the United States can call or visit the website to request a free catalog and card samples. Residents of Canada can request a free catalog and card samples online.

Web Resources for Parents

The World Wide Web is a fantastic source of information and other resources for parents. Where else can you chat with other new parents from around the world with a click of the mouse, get up-to-date on the latest parenting information—even find out what to do when your child gets a carrot stuck up her nose!

The websites that I have listed in this chapter are exceptional parenting websites that all offer something of great interest to new or expecting Web-friendly parents—websites that you will definitely want to bookmark!

You could easily spend several hours on these websites, chatting with other new parents, participating in discussion boards, browsing through tons of parenting articles, hooking up with other moms and dads in your own area, getting support and advice or the latest medical, first-aid, and child safety information—you name it! There are even games, quizzes, and activities just for parents to keep you entertained for hours!

General Parenting Resources

The following websites contain general parenting information, on subjects such as pregnancy and childbirth, breast-feeding, and caring for your baby.

❀ **Adoption.com**

U.S. website: www.adoption.com
Canadian website: www.canadianadoption.com

Adoption.com is committed to helping children find loving, permanent homes. They also assist adoptees and birthparents to find birth families. Their website offers a photo listing of waiting children, a place where parents can list their profile online, an adoption reunion registry, and various other services.

❀ **Babies Today**

www.babiestoday.com

The Babies Today website includes discussion boards, Q&As with experts, and tips on lifestyle issues like maternity fashion and finance management.

❀ **Baby Bag**

www.babybag.com

This parenting website features many pregnancy and childbirth stories, articles, product recalls, and parenting information.

❀ **Canadian Childcare Directory**

www.childcaredirectory.com

The Canadian Childcare Directory is a fun and easy-to-use directory that includes more than eight thousand listings for both parents and child care providers. You can search the interactive, user-friendly directory by entering your province, your city, and the first three digits of your postal code to find child care and educational facilities in your area. This is a Canadian service that is available free of charge, 24/7.

❀ **Canadian Parents Online**

www.canadianparents.com

At Canadian Parents Online you'll find numerous parenting articles, a free newsletter, a moms club, nutritious recipes, as well as access to a panel of experts that includes pediatricians, dieticians, childbirth educators, and others.

❀ Cycle Daily
www.cycledaily.com/download.htm

Charting your fertility signs can help you predict or recognize when you are the most fertile. Visit the above-listed website to download a fertility chart and learn how to record your fertility signs.

❀ FamilyFun
www.family.com

This creative Disney site features activities and crafts, parenting articles, expert advice, thousands of family ideas and activities, games and recipes, and more. There is a multitude of stuff for moms, dads, and kids of all ages.

❀ Fisher-Price
www.fisher-price.com/us/myfp

The Fisher-Price website offers the *Grow-with-Me Parenting Guide* with information about your child's development, as well as help in finding the right toy or activity to stimulate your child. This guide covers the first month to the fifth year of a child's life, and beyond.

❀ Get My Child Support
www.getmychildsupport.com

According to this informative site, more than sixteen million custodial parents are not receiving their court-ordered child support payments. This site offers a free Do-It Yourself Guide to help you collect money owed to you for child support, as well as free information on a service that will locate missing parents and collect and enforce court-ordered support payments. Visit this site to download the appropriate guides and forms to collect child support.

❀ International Childbirth Education Association
www.icea.org

The International Childbirth Education Association is available to help parents find birth professionals in their hometown, including childbirth educators, postnatal educators, certified doulas, and perinatal fitness educators. This service is available to residents of the United States and Canada.

❀ Johnson's Baby
www.johnsonsbaby.com/learning_place/step_by_step

This Johnson & Johnson's website offers numerous printable step-by-step guides and excellent how-to videos you can view online to learn how to care for your new baby. The following topics are covered in these guides and instructional videos: *Bathing Your Baby*; *Breast-Feeding Your Baby*; *Holding Your Baby, Dressing Your Baby, and More*; *Caring for Your Baby's Skin*; *Massage Your Baby*; and *Bonding with Your Baby*.

❀ KittyBids
www.familyauction.com

The KittyBids website is an online auction where moms can get great deals on baby clothing, furniture, and other baby items and accessories.

❀ Lamaze International
In the United States or Canada, call 800-368-4404
www.lamaze-childbirth.com (click on "For Expectant and New
   Parents")

The mission of Lamaze International is to promote, support, and protect normal birth through education and advocacy. The Lamaze website provides information on selecting a childbirth education class, tips for a healthy pregnancy, and pregnancy-related articles. If you are an expectant parent looking for a Lamaze childbirth education class, use the online Locator Service or call and ask to speak with a representative.

Male Infertility
www.urologychannel.com/maleinfertility/index.shtml

This site offers current facts on male infertility with information on possible causes, risk factors, treatment, and more. Many other resources are also available at this informative site.

National Adoption Foundation
www.nafadopt.org

The National Adoption Foundation is a national organization that provides financial support and information and services for adoptive families, before, during, and after their adoptions are finalized. The foundation also offers grants and loans to help families finance adoption.

National Parenting Center
www.tnpc.com

The National Parenting Center provides parents with responsible guidance from the world's most renowned child-rearing authorities. The organization also offers product reviews, children's craft ideas, and more.

Parenthood.com
www.parenthood.com

This excellent all-purpose parenting site covers all areas of parenting and childbirth. You'll find a list of baby names, an ovulation calculator, a due date calculator, and more.

❧ Parents' Action for Children

www.parentsaction.org

Founded by Rob Reiner, Parents' Action for Children is the voice of American parents whose goal is to bring parents together to change the nation's policies for children and families. Visit the website to have your voice heard in national policy debates affecting children and families. With just the click of a mouse, you can send messages to the president and state and national legislators on matters important to children, including early education, health care, and child care.

❧ Parents Canada

www.parentscanada.com

From the publishers of *Expecting, Best Wishes,* and *Parents Canada* magazines, the Parents Canada website has tons of valuable information on pregnancy, labor, and birth. They offer lots of help in caring for a healthy, happy, and safe child, as well as current information on your baby's growth and development in the first year, nutrition, sleep, and more. Leading health and medical authorities in Canada supply all the information on this website.

❧ Parents' Choice Foundation

www.parents-choice.org

Parents' Choice offers hundreds of online reviews and resources for parents and others who are involved in the lives of children. You will find information about children's toys, as well as help in making informed decisions about which products are right for your children.

❧ Parents.com

www.parents.com

This excellent parenting website contains tons of information for new or expecting moms, covering foods that are off-limits during pregnancy, false labor, dangerous herbs and medications, exercising safely during pregnancy, and pregnancy first aid. Also available are free newsletters and articles, as well as age-by-age advice on every stage as your child grows.

✿ Parents Helping Parents: The Parent-Directed Family Resource Center for Children with Special Needs
www.php.com

This parent-directed family resource center is available for parents of children with physical, emotional, mental, or learning disabilities. It is run for and by parents of children with special needs. The online library provides many resources for special needs children.

✿ Parent Soup
www.parentsoup.com

One of the best parenting sites around, Parent Soup deals with issues relating to children of all ages. The site offers a developmental tracker, discussion boards, parenting workshops for women, articles written by pediatric experts, chats, message boards, quizzes, and more.

✿ ParentsPlace.com
www.parentsplace.com

This website is a good starting point to find out current information on all areas of pregnancy and childbirth, as well as parenting of all ages and stages. At this site you can also find bulletin boards and chats, advice from the experts, pregnancy and due date calendars, baby name finders, and more.

✿ Parentstages.com
www.parentstages.com

Powered by Huggies, Parentstages.com offers tools to help you create a personalized birth plan, search for the perfect baby name, and follow the daily development of your baby from conception to birth. You

can also get advice on childproofing every corner of your home and read
articles on numerous other parenting topics.

✖ Preconception.com
www.preconception.com

Preconception.com is a website of practical resources for those trying to conceive, with up-to-date information on conception, fertility
charts, an ovulation calculator, and more.

✖ Pregnancy by the Numbers Checklists

At these Parents.com websites for the expecting mom, you can print
out a first, second, or third trimester to-do list, a handy reminder list of
the things you will want to do throughout the different stages of your
pregnancy.

First Trimester To-Do List:
www.parents.com/articles/pregnancy/1133.jsp

Second Trimester To-Do List:
www.parents.com/articles/pregnancy/1134.jsp

Third Trimester To-Do List:
www.parents.com/articles/pregnancy/1135.jsp

✖ Safe Stay USA
www.safestayusa.com

Planning a trip with your little one? Safe Stay USA offers a convenient directory to help you find a hotel or motel that is baby-friendly and
safe for your little one on the move. This service is available to residents
of the United States only.

✖ Today's Parent
www.todaysparent.com

The Today's Parent website provides free contests, quizzes, craft ideas, recipes for kids, book reviews, forums, features, and details on upcoming special events. You can create a digital family photo album to share photos of your family with others. Click on "Parenting A–Z" to access the Today's Parent Library, where you can find numerous articles addressed to specific ages of children, birth and pregnancy-related articles, and more.

❦ Zero to Three
www.zerotothree.org

Zero to Three is a nonprofit organization whose goal is to promote healthy development of infants and toddlers from birth to age three. It is the nation's leading resource on the first three years of life. The website offers great resources for parents, including parenting tips, articles, information on early literacy, and more. At www.zerotothree.org/brainwonders you can learn some fascinating facts about how the brain develops from conception to three years of age.

Health and Medical Resources

As each situation is unique, the medical information provided in these websites should not be used as a substitute for the medical care and personal attention of your physician or for any emergency situations. There may be variations in treatment that your physician may recommend, based on individual facts and circumstances. The information in these websites is available solely to educate you and arm you with the types of questions you will need to ask your doctor in an attempt to better prepare you for your child's next doctor's visit.

❦ American Academy of Pediatrics
www.aap.org

The American Academy of Pediatrics is dedicated to the health, safety, and well-being of infants, children, adolescents, and young adults.

The organization's website offers a wealth of information on such topics as child health and nutrition, immunizations, children with disabilities, and everything you need to know to keep your child healthy.

🎀 American Dental Association
www.ada.org/public/media/videos/psa/index.asp

The American Dental Association offers thirty-second videotaped or animated messages to help teach your little one to start brushing her teeth. These cute online minivideos include *Baby Digby's First Tooth*, *Baby Bottle Tooth Decay*, *Healthy Snacks with Dudley*, *Dudley's Dental Quiz*, and more. Great for when baby's first teeth start to appear!

🎀 Canadian Paediatric Society
www.caringforkids.cps.ca

Caring for Kids is a Canadian website developed by the Canadian Paediatric Society. This site was designed to provide parents with information about their children's health and well-being. All information provided at this website is reviewed by a committee of experts. Topics covered include "Pregnancy and Babies," "When Your Child Is Sick," "Healthy Eating," "Immunization," "Keeping Your Child Healthy," and more. This website is also available in the French language.

🎀 Children's Tylenol and Children's Motrin Dosing Charts
www.getwellkids.com (click on "Dosing Charts")

Visit the website for a printable dosing chart for Children's Tylenol and Children's Motrin, arranged according to a child's weight and age, to be sure you give your child the right dose every time.

🎀 KidsHealth
www.kidshealth.org

The KidsHealth website is a great site for parents who have questions about their kids' illnesses. It also contains a multitude of articles on pregnancy and childbirth.

🌸 March of Dimes
www.modimes.org

For more than sixty-four years, the March of Dimes, through its programs and research, has saved millions of babies from death or disability. In addition, the organization helps moms and babies get access to health care. The website contains valuable information for new or expecting parents on infant health, birth defects, the importance of folic acid, premature births, and the importance of prenatal care, as well as numerous other articles on pregnancy and parenting.

🌸 Mayo Clinic
www.mayoclinic.com (click on "Healthy Living")

Tap into the expertise of one of the world's most renowned medical research institutions, the Mayo Clinic, to find valuable medical information on common problems of children and on pediatric conditions, as well as medical quizzes. The Healthy Living centers offer a collection of information and tools on baby's health, children's health, food and nutrition, pregnancy, women's health, and more.

🌸 *The Merck Manual of Medical Information—Home Edition*
www.merckhomeedition.com/home.html

The Merck Manual, written by nearly two hundred leading medical experts, is a best-selling medical reference that has sold more than two million copies worldwide. It contains complete and in-depth medical information about diseases, diagnosis, prevention and treatment, and more. Visit the website to view the interactive version or the text-based version, both available free of charge and written in easy-to-understand English. A great page to bookmark!

🌸 Postpartum Stress Center
www.postpartumstress.com

The Postpartum Stress Center specializes in the treatment of postpartum illnesses. Its website offers information on postpartum depression, including self-help suggestions on things that can make you feel better, as well as information on where you can get help, support groups, grief counseling, and more.

❦ Postpartum Support International
www.chss.iup.edu/postpartum

Postpartum Support International provides social support and information regarding postpartum mood disorders and depression. The website offers postpartum chat rooms and bulletin boards. There are online self-assessment surveys for moms who are depressed or stressed, as well as information about anxiety and panic attacks, postpartum fatigue, exhaustion, and more.

❦ UnitedHealth Foundation
www.unitedhealthfoundation.org

This website provides information on becoming more knowledgeable about your own health and your health care options, as well as information on how to be a smarter health care consumer.

Child Safety and First Aid

Every parent should visit and bookmark the websites in this section to become familiar with first-aid procedures, the basics of infant and child CPR, and what to do in case of an emergency. What you learn at these sites may save your child's life!

❦ Band-Aid
www.bandaid.com/first_aid_guide.shtml

At the Band-Aid website you can download a free printable *First Aid Guide* with basic emergency information on many first-aid topics, such as shock, frostbite, sunburn, chemical burns, and unconsciousness.

✿ Canadian Consumer Information Gateway
www.consumerinformation.ca (click on "Safety")

This site provides a vast amount of reliable safety information from Government of Canada departments and agencies. Some of the many topics covered are food safety, household safety, medication, and product safety and recalls.

✿ Childbirth Solutions, Inc.
www.childbirthsolutions.com/articles/postpartum.php

This informative website will help you learn the basics of infant CPR, emergency care that is given to a baby who has stopped breathing. This website also covers such important topics as newborn circumcision, immunization, newborn care, newborn complications, postpartum health, SIDS, and colic.

✿ Clue in to Safety
www.clueintosafety.com

Clue in to Safety is a safety project brought to you by Ford, in cooperation with Blue's Clues, to help you and your children learn important safety lessons. Click on "Visit the Front Seat for Parents!" for valuable information on vehicle safety, home safety, fire safety, water safety, and police safety. This website also offers children's safety games, printable coloring pages, and a free poster.

✿ DaimlerChrysler SeatCheck
In the United States, call 866-SEAT-CHECK
www.seatcheck.org

At this website you can search for a listing of child passenger safety seat inspection locations nationwide, where inspectors can provide guidance on proper child restraint use and installation. Visit the website or call to find an inspection location near you. This program is available to residents of the United States only.

❧ Enfamil Baby Essentials

www.enfamil.com/baby_care/baby_essentials/e_1_2.html

This informative website will provide you with safety tips on the following topics: car seat safety, baby carriers, backpacks, front packs, stroller safety, and more.

❧ Juvenile Products Manufacturers Association

www.jpma.org

This website informs consumers about the safe use of juvenile products and industry issues. Information is available to help you in selecting safe juvenile products for your children. During your visit to the website, make sure you check out the "Baby Safety" section, which presents valuable information on providing a safe environment for your baby in the kitchen, bedroom, living room, carport, and bath.

❧ KidsHealth

www.kidshealth.org/parent/firstaid_safe/index.html

This website covers tons of first-aid topics, including emergencies, home safety and first aid, safety away from the home, and outdoors and seasonal safety.

❧ Parents.com

www.parents.com

This website is an excellent resource for first-aid and safety instructions. All new or expecting parents should visit this website to become familiar with what to do in case of an emergency. Some of the topics covered include what to do if your child is choking, what foods can cause choking in young children, how to tell if your child's case is urgent, when to call 911, baby safety basics, and more. The following informative articles can be viewed online:

- "Baby Safety Basics." www.parents.com/articles/health/2037
  .jsp. This article covers such important topics as bathtub safety
  and drowning, choking, falls, car seat mistakes, and more.
- "Burn Danger Checklist." www.parents.com/articles/health/
  2084.jsp. Take these simple steps throughout the house to
  protect your child from burn-related injuries.
- "Checklist: 10 First-Aid Must-Haves (for Cuts)." www.parents
  .com/articles/health/2102.jsp. This is a handy checklist of the
  ten emergency essentials to have readily available to treat your
  child's cuts and scrapes.
- "Checklist: Top Food Hazards." www.parents.com/articles/
  health/2099.jsp. This is a listing of foods to avoid giving your
  child since they may cause choking.
- "Fire Prevention Checklist." www.parents.com/articles/health/
  2090.jsp. Provided are precautions that you can take throughout
  your house to reduce the risk of fire.
- "First Aid for Burns and Scalds." www.parents.com/
  articles/health/2059.jsp. Kids under the age of five are at
  greater risk for burns because they don't understand the con-
  sequences of fire and heat. This section covers first-, second-,
  and third-degree burns and what you can do to save your
  child's skin.
- "First Aid for Choking." www.parents.com/articles/health/
  2060.jsp. Provided are life-saving tips, including what to do in
  an emergency, how to save a choking child under one year of
  age, and how to save an older child who is choking.
- "First Aid for Cuts and Bleeding." www.parents.com/articles/
  health/2061.jsp. Check out this website for instructions on
  treating your child's cuts, bruises, and bleeding.
- "First-Aid Kit Essentials." www.parents.com/articles/health/
  2052.jsp. Included is a handy checklist of first-aid kit essentials
  to keep in your at-home first-aid kit.
- "First Aid on Vacation." www.parents.com/articles/health/
  2126.jsp. This article discusses how to prevent injuries and treat
  illnesses when away from home on vacation.

- "Over-the-Counter Medication Guide." www.parents.com/ articles/health/2064.jsp. Don't give your child the wrong dose of a common medicine. Check out this guide for proper dosage instructions.
- "Strangulation and Suffocation." www.parents.com/articles/ health/2065.jsp. This article explains what to do to prevent strangulation and suffocation and what to do in case of such emergencies.
- "Treating Baby Bites." www.parents.com/articles/health/ 2080.jsp. Information is provided on what to do if another child bites your little one.
- "When to Call 911." www.parents.com/articles/health/2036.jsp. This article offers information on how you can tell if your child's case is urgent and when you should call 911.

Safe Kids
www.safekids.org

The National Safe Kids Campaign is dedicated to preventing the number-one killer of children fourteen and younger—unintentional injury. At the Safe Kids website, you'll find more than five hundred ways to keep your children safe, including information on how to safely wear a bike helmet, how to properly install a child car seat, and more. To learn more about this campaign and how to keep your children safe, visit the website.

Safe Kids Canada
www.safekidscanada.ca (click on "Safety Tips to Keep Kids Safe")

Safe Kids Canada is a terrific website that offers a multitude of ways to help keep kids safe. Topics covered include safety tips for children under the age of five, airline travel safety, water safety, winter safety, first-aid instructions, and more. The website also offers home safety, road safety, and playground safety checklists.

❀ **U.S. Consumer Product Safety Commission**
www.cpsc.gov

The goal of the U.S. Consumer Product Safety Commission is to help keep families safe by reducing the risk of death or injury from consumer products. This website provides you with a list of products that have been recalled; it reports unsafe products as well.

Resources for Parents of Multiples

Being a parent of multiples brings about unique challenges and experiences, beginning with the pregnancy of multiples as well as the labor and delivery of multiples, then on to coordinating nursing, feeding, and sleeping schedules—and trying to get your babies on the same schedules. The following websites offer articles, tips, and support groups, as well as advice from other parents of multiples.

❀ **National Organization of Mothers of Twins Club**
www.nomotc.org

NOMOTC promotes the special aspects of child development that relate to multiple-birth children. The website will connect you to local twin and multiples clubs.

❀ **Parents of Multiples Across Canada**
www.mom2many.com

This Internet community for Canadian parents of multiples offers forums, resources, birth stories, chats, articles, and more.

❀ *Twins*
www.twinsmagazine.com

The *Twins* magazine website provides great resources for parents of twins and multiples, including information on nursing and feeding your multiples, message boards, and numerous other great resources.

❀ **Twinsworld.com**
   www.twinsworld.com

This website features twin festival information, twin merchandise, bulletin boards, chats, and jokes for parents of multiples, as well as links to other multiples' websites.

Preemie Parenting Resources

A quarter of a million babies are born prematurely every year in the United States alone. As premature infants will often need special care, I have listed the following websites, which deal with the challenges and complications faced by parents with premature infants. These websites offer support groups, resources, and articles, as well as inspirational stories from parents of preemies.

❀ **Baby Place**
   www.baby-place.com/premature.htm

This website contains many links to support groups, resources, and articles for parents of premature infants. You can find resources dealing with how to care for your premature baby, miracle birth stories, preemie chats, and more.

❀ **Preemie Page**
   www.motherstuff.com/html/preemie.htm

At this website, parents of preemies will find links to interesting articles, preemie health information, support groups, and other Internet resources.

❀ **Preemie Parenting**
   www.preemieparenting.com

Preemie Parenting is a place created for parents and loved ones of premature infants, as well as for women experiencing a high-risk or complicated pregnancy. The site offers access to information, support, and resources. You can read preemie birth stories and inspirational pieces, and you can learn about infant medical complications, problems, and special needs, as well as medical causes of prematurity. Also provided is a list of parenting support groups.

For Moms

The following resources are available for all kinds of moms: single moms, stay-at-home moms, and working moms. Speaking of stay-at-home and working moms, at this point in the book I just thought I'd take some time out to vent a bit—hope you don't mind! Stay-at-home moms, working moms—we're all moms, doing our best to raise our children. I've been both a stay-at-home mom as well as a working mom. My children never stopped loving me when I decided to go back to work. In fact, our relationship was just as close as ever and never suffered in the least.

I'm becoming tired of people who judge you as a parent because you decide to work outside of the home or because you choose to stay at home with your children. The most important thing is the quality time that you do spend with your children when you're with them, and that you give them all the love, support, and encouragement they need.

So let's stop wasting our time judging each other and concentrate on the things in life that are a true concern—the children who really do need special help and attention, such as children who are abused, neglected, or homeless. Okay, moving right along. . . .

BlueSuitMom.com
www.bluesuitmom.com

This website for working moms offers practical tips on balancing work and home. You'll find tips for planning meals, travel, and managing time, as well as information on working from home, women-owned businesses, and ways to find time for the family. Ideas for family activities are also provided.

❦ FitMommies.com
www.fitmommies.com

For the active mom, this website features workouts and exercises for all levels of fitness, activities and information for active families, nutrition information, healthy recipes, and more.

❦ National Organization of Single Mothers
www.singlemothers.org

There are thirteen million single mothers in the United States. Single parents now make up the majority of households. This website provides a great support system for single moms, helping single mothers get in touch with other single moms and offering help and advice for successfully raising your children. Single mothers can find articles, tips, and advice to help them deal with the day-to-day challenges of single parenting.

❦ National Women's Health Information Center
www.4women.gov

The National Women's Health Information Center offers information on a wide variety of women's health-related issues, including pregnancy, postpartum depression, breast cancer, breast-feeding, nutrition, contraception and gynecology, abuse, and general women's health concerns.

❦ SingleRose.com
www.singlerose.com

SingleRose.com is for single mothers who are raising their children alone. The site offers discussion boards, chats, and articles on single parenting. Some of the topics covered at this site include divorce recovery, dealing with anger, child support, and custody issues.

❀ Single Young Moms' Mailing List
http://members.tripod.com/~SingleMoms

For the young mom, this mailing list offers single young (twenty-five and under) moms a place to meet new people and share experiences, advice, and friendship.

❀ Stay at Home Mom
www.stayathomemom.com

The Stay at Home Mom website was designed to create a positive place for stay-at-home moms to gather and encourage each other. The forum-driven website contains a message board where you can read and post messages, read articles, and more.

For Dads

For the Web-friendly dads who want to connect with other dads, obtain up-to-date parenting information, sharpen their cooking skills, read articles, and get advice from other fathers, these terrific fathering websites are for you! They suggest all kinds of activities you can do together with your kids, offer help and advice for the stay-at-home dad, feature father-friendly chats, and more.

❀ Center for Successful Fathering
www.fathering.org

This website has a self-assessment test for dads, as well as numerous links to other fathering websites. Information is available to provide dads with skills and resources to assist them in becoming the best dads they can be!

❧ Fathers Network

www.fathersnetwork.org

This website presents a wealth of resources and information for fathers, including father support groups, organizations, and more. The mission of the Fathers Network is to support fathers and families who are raising children with special needs and developmental disabilities.

❧ Father's World

www.fathersworld.com

Dads will have access here to resources pertaining to many areas of interest, such as support and parenting education, health, recipes, news, and legal issues. The goal of Father's World is to connect fathers with each other and with various support agencies and associations.

❧ National Center for Fathering

www.fathers.com

This fathering website provides practical, how-to–oriented resources to prepare dads for nearly every fathering situation. It is a great resource for dads seeking to strengthen their fathering skills. Fathers can sign up at the National Center for Fathering to receive *Fathers.Com Weekly*, a free weekly newsletter delivered via e-mail.

❧ Parenthub

www.parenthub.com/parenting/father.htm

This website contains links to magazines, articles, and resources for single dads, stepdads, and divorced dads. Dads will have access to discipline tips for single dads, studies of children in fatherless homes, and advice from other fathers.

🎞 Slowlane.com
www.slowlane.com

Slowlane.com offers stay-at-home dads a wide variety of online references, resources, and links to other fathering sites. The website provides dads with a searchable collection of articles and media clips written by, for, and about primary caregiving fathers.

Free Online Medical Advice

At the following medical websites, highly respected doctors, pediatricians, and other medical experts are available to answer your medical and parenting questions. Just type in your question at the website, and these professionals will do their best to answer you in a timely fashion.

These websites offer a wealth of free medical advice and information for parents, as well as a chance to view tons of medical-related articles. Topics covered include pregnancy, labor and birth, newborn issues, pregnancy complications, prenatal health, nutrition, breast-feeding, children's health, growth and development, pediatric illnesses, and more.

Please note: These online doctors and medical experts will try their very best to answer all of your medical questions. But because many of these medical websites receive hundreds, even thousands, of questions each week, they may not always be able to answer each and every question individually. For these reasons, many of the websites have posted online Q&As in different medical categories, which you can view to look for an answer to your question. You may want to check out these posted Q&As first before you ask the doctor a question.

As each situation is unique, the medical information provided in these websites should not be used as a substitute for the medical care and personal attention of your physician or for any emergency situations. There may be variations in treatment that your physician may recommend, based on individual facts and circumstances. The information in these websites is available solely to educate you and arm you with the types of questions you will need to ask your doctor in an attempt to better prepare you for your next doctor's visit.

❦ AllExperts.com
www.allexperts.com

AllExperts.com, the oldest and largest free Q&A service on the Internet, has thousands of volunteer experts available to answer your questions. Just pick a category, click, and ask a question. Categories include everything from arts and humanities to television and radio. There are too many topics to list! The "parenting/family" category covers such areas as adoption, day care, pregnancy and birth, fatherhood, grandparenting, single parents, stay-at-home parents, parenting special needs children, parenting multiples, parenting babies and toddlers, and children's books.

❦ Answers from Mayo Clinic
www.mayoclinic.com/findinformation/answers/index.cfm

Specialists from the Mayo Clinic will answer your medical questions in a wide range of categories, including food and nutrition, mental health, pregnancy and reproduction, women's health, children's conditions, and other pregnancy-related concerns. As these specialists receive thousands of questions each week, they cannot answer all of them, but you can view their posted Q&As online in the many different categories as listed above.

❦ Ask Dr. Sears
www.parenting.com/parenting/experts/sears/index.html

Dr. Sears is a leading pediatrician and the author of more than twenty-five books on child care. You can view his responses to new concerns every day on his special message board or ask him a question at the website.

❦ Ask the Dietitian
www.dietitian.com/index.html

A registered dietitian is available to answer your nutrition questions in the following categories: infants and toddlers, food allergies, calories, eating habits, and more. The online dietitian will read your e-mail and try to answer your questions in a timely fashion.

❦ Ask the Immunization Experts
www.immunize.org/catg.d/p2021.htm

At this website you can view immunization-related questions and answers concerning diphtheria, tetanus, pertussis, polio, measles, mumps, rubella, and other such diseases.

❦ Ask the Pediatrician
www.keepkidshealthy.com/ask_the_pediatrician.html

At KeepKidsHealthy.com you can ask the pediatrician questions about your children's health, growth, and development, as well as about their symptoms and illnesses.

❦ Ask the Pros
www.childbirth.org/AskANurse/pros.html

At this medical website you can ask a childbirth educator questions about pregnancy, labor, and birth; ask a doula questions about the basics of pregnancy, birth, and breast-feeding; ask a lactation consultant questions about breast-feeding; ask a midwife questions about homebirth and midwifery; or ask a nurse questions about fertility and pregnancy.

❦ Call Your Pediatrician
www.callyourped.com

This website provides information on common illnesses and how they can be safely treated, as well as advice on when to call the doctor, home medical treatments, and more. Among the illnesses covered are asthma, chickenpox, coughs and colds, croup, diaper rash, dehydration, ear and eye infections, fever, and vomiting.

❧ Child Behavioral Health Forum
www.medhelp.org (click on "Child Behavior")

At this Med Help International forum, doctors from Harvard Vanguard Medical Associates will answer questions about child discipline, child behavior management, normal child development, and more.

❧ Dr. Paul's Child Health and Wellness Info Site
www.drpaul.com

Dr. Paul is a highly respected Canadian pediatrician. At this site, you can ask the doctor a question or search through a multitude of Dr. Paul's articles relating to different parenting topics, such as newborn issues, growth and development, nutrition, breast-feeding, and other child health and wellness issues.

❧ Dr. Spock Company
www.drspock.com (click on "Ask Our Experts")

When you register online as a Dr. Spock user, you can submit a question, which will then be directed to the right expert. There are all types of experts available at this website who will answer as many questions as possible in categories such as pregnancy and birth, pediatric behavior and development, infectious diseases, and childhood immunizations.

❧ Earlychildhood.com
www.earlychildhood.com (click on "Ask Our Experts")

The specialists available at this website will deal with such early childhood concerns as binkies, blankies, bottles, potty training, and bed-wetting.

❦ Pediatric Neurosurgery
www.nyneurosurgery.org

At this Institute for Neurology and Neurosurgery website, you can view topics relating to pediatric neurosurgery, including spina bifida and cerebral palsy, as well as ask the doctor neurological questions.

❦ Vascular Birthmarks Foundation
www.birthmark.org/ask_the_doctor.php

Here you can ask the doctor questions about your child's birthmark, including hemangiomas, port wine stains, and other vascular malformations.

Free Government
Resources for New or
Expecting Parents

The government offers a wealth of free resources to new or expecting parents, including parenting publications and other literature, programs that offer free financial assistance and nutritional foods to parents, and various tax breaks and other benefits to help parents with the cost of raising a child.

Take the time to familiarize yourself with what is available from the government, as listed throughout this chapter.

Free Publications

The informative publications listed in this section are free and readily available to you as a parent. Simply call or go online to request those publications that are of interest to you.

❧ Government of Canada Publications
In Canada, call 800-O-CANADA

Call the Government of Canada to request any of the following free publications. Calls are answered personally in the caller's choice of either English or French. Phone lines are open Monday to Friday, 8 A.M. to 8 P.M. EST. (Those who are hearing impaired can call the Government of Canada at 800-465-7735 to order these free publications.)

• *10 Valuable Tips for Successful Breastfeeding.* This informative pamphlet, aimed at new mothers, covers the basics of breast-feeding.

• *Back to Sleep.* SIDS is less common in babies who sleep on their backs. This pamphlet, which is also available at www.back-to-sleep.com, explains the correct sleeping positions for infants, as well as other important facts that you need to know to reduce the risk of SIDS and suffocation.

• *Canada's Food Guide to Healthy Eating.* This booklet offers practical guidelines you can use daily to make healthy food choices for you and your family.

• *International Adoption and the Immigration Process.* This booklet is designed to serve as a guide to the process of international adoption and the entry of adoptive children into Canada. It outlines the basic steps and procedures that must be followed. This publication can be ordered online at ww.cic.gc.ca/english/sponsor/adopt%2D4.html.

• *Is Your Child Safe?* Injury is the leading cause of death among children and youth in Canada. Many of these injuries occur at home. This publication informs parents how they can make their environment safer for their children. It covers home safety, fire safety, emergency preparedness, and more.

• *Keep Kids Safe.* This publication discusses child safety, including the proper use of car seats and booster seats, child restraint recalls, and more.

⚘ **HRSA (Health Resources and Services Administration) Information Center**
In the United States, call 888-AskHRSA
www.ask.hrsa.gov/search.cfm

The following publications are available free of charge from the HRSA Information Center of the U.S. Department of Health and Human Services. To order a free single copy of a publication, call, or visit the website.

• *Bright Futures Family Pocket Guide: Raising Healthy Infants, Children, and Adolescents.* This guide is written especially for families to prepare them to become better partners for their children's health. It highlights important child health topics, including what will happen at a health visit from birth to age twenty-one, how your child grows, and what to expect when your child gets older. Also featured are family websites, resources for families, tip sheets, and more. Order by Inventory Code Number MCHN022.

• *Bright Futures for Families: Lead Poisoning.* This booklet contains information on lead poisoning in children. It informs the public about lead poisoning, its causes, and its problems. The booklet will show you how you can protect your children from lead poisoning at home and at school. Order by Inventory Code Number MCHM067.

• *Health Diary: Myself My Baby.* Developed to help expectant mothers have a healthy baby, this ninety-four-page health diary contains formatted pages to complete for prenatal and newborn pediatric appointments. In addition, this diary contains information on fetal development, child development, prenatal care, pregnancy, and newborn care. Order by Inventory Code Number MCHH064.

• *Newborn Screening: State Policy Directions and Trends.* This informative newsletter talks about the newborn screening laws enacted in the 1960s and 1970s and the advances in the area of genetic sciences. Order by Inventory Code Number MCHN069.

- *Paying the Bills: Tips for Families on Financing Health Care for Children with Special Needs.* This booklet includes tips in the following areas: getting started, making your child's health insurance work for your family, making public programs work for you, tackling medical bills, influencing decision makers, documenting your child's special needs, cost savings, finding other sources of funding, and connecting with other families. Order by Inventory Code Number MCHL094.

- *Vaccination Cards for Health Diary: Myself, My Baby.* These cards provide updated vaccination guidelines for use with *Health Diary: Myself, My Baby* (listed earlier). Order by Inventory Code Number MCHN121.

- *Working and Breastfeeding: Can You Do It? Yes, You Can!* This booklet contains useful information for mothers who may be returning to work while they are still breast-feeding. It explains the benefits of breast-feeding for mother and baby and how to fit breast-feeding into a working mother's schedule. Order by Inventory Code Number MCHL007.

❧ National Adoption Information Clearinghouse
http://naic.acf.hhs.gov

Established by Congress in 1987, the National Adoption Information Clearinghouse (NAIC) provides free information on all aspects of adoption, including domestic and intercountry adoption. The clearinghouse offers a number of adoption information packages and numerous adoption-related publications, too many to mention, on all areas of adoption. Log on to the website for a listing of free publications.

❧ National Center for Missing and Exploited Children
In the United States or Canada, call 800-843-5678 (ask for
    booklet #12)
www.ncmec.org
Call to receive the free safety booklet *Just in Case . . . Parental Guidelines in Case You Need a Babysitter*, with safety tips, information on find-

ing and hiring a babysitter, and more. You can also call if you have information on missing or exploited children. This offer is available to residents of the United States and Canada.

🎀 National Center on Birth Defects and Developmental Disabilities
In the United States, call 888-232-5929

Call for a free booklet on folic acid and its role in preventing birth defects. This offer is available to residents of the United States only.

🎀 U.S. Consumer Product Safety Commission
In the United States or Canada, call 800-638-2772
www.cpsc.gov/cpscpub/pubs/pub_idx.html

The following U.S. Consumer Product Safety Commission publications are available free of charge. You can request them by calling or visiting the website.

• *Baby Product Safety Alert.* This publication discusses strangulation, suffocation, and other hazards in the use of cribs, crib toys, strollers, bunk beds, plastic bags, rattles, and more. Order CPSC Document #250.

• *Baby Safety Shower How-To Kit.* If you're looking for ways to help parents take better care of their children by giving them new ideas about keeping their babies safe at home, consider organizing a baby safety shower for yourself or for an expectant friend. A baby safety shower is a learning party where all the activities revolve around home safety themes. Everyone attending the shower will learn tips to keep their children safe. The U.S. Consumer Product Safety Commission and Gerber Products Company developed this baby safety shower initiative to help good parents become even better ones. The materials you'll need to get started are included in this kit. Also provided is a Baby Safety Checklist, which can be used as a growth chart to help you watch your baby grow. Order CPSC Document #207.

- *Child Care Safety Checklist for Parents and Child Care Providers.* Use the safety tips provided in this handy checklist to help keep your children safe. Topics include choosing a crib, safety gates, bedding, window blind and curtain cords, and more. Order CPSC Document #242.

- *Childproofing Your Home.* This booklet lists twelve safety devices to protect your children, such as window guards, safety latches and locks, safety gates, and outlet covers. Order CPSC Document #202.

- *For Kids' Sake: Think Toy Safety.* This publication covers toy safety, as well as buying, maintaining, and storing infants' and children's toys. Order CPSC Document #281.

- *Tips for Your Baby's Safety.* This publication contains a Nursery Equipment Safety Checklist to help you when buying new or secondhand nursery equipment. It can also be used when checking over nursery equipment in your home or in other facilities that care for infants and young children. Order CPSC Document #200.

- *Which Toy for Which Child: Birth to 5 Years of Age.* This is a consumers' guide for selecting suitable toys for infants and children from birth to age five. Order CPSC Document #285.

Free Financial Assistance, Tax Breaks, and Other Benefits in the United States

The government offers assistance to families with children in various ways, including financial assistance and support services for low-income families, health insurance programs, food and nutrition programs, as well as beneficial tax credits to those who are eligible. Please review the following listings for more information on these programs and services and their eligibility requirements.

❧ Adoption Credit
www.irs.gov/formspubs (type "Topic 607" in the Search box)

To help offset the costs involved in adoption, adoptive parents can claim a tax credit for up to $10,000 for qualifying expenses paid to adopt a child. Qualifying expenses include adoption fees, court costs, legal fees, traveling, and other necessary expenses. Visit the website for more information on this benefit.

❦ Centers for Medicare and Medicaid Services

In the United States, call 410-786-3000 (sorry, not a toll-free number)

www.hcfa.gov/medicaid

Medicaid is a joint federal and state program that provides health insurance and medical assistance to approximately forty million low-income Americans. It is the single largest provider of family planning services to women of reproductive health age. Nationwide, about 40 percent of all births are funded by Medicaid, as many pregnant women can qualify for it even if their income is greater than the federal poverty level. Without the Medicaid program, millions of women and their children would be left with no health insurance at all. The Medicaid program varies considerably from state to state, as each state establishes its own eligibility standards and administers its own program. At http://cms .hhs.gov/medicaid/mcontact.asp you will find state Medicaid contacts, as well as state-by-state Medicaid toll-free numbers where you can contact your state Medicaid officials for details about the Medicaid program in your state. For more information about Medicaid eligibility, Medicaid services, and how to apply for Medicaid, go online or call the Centers for Medicare and Medicaid Services. For a listing of phone numbers of local Medicaid offices, you can also call 800-633-4227.

❦ Child Care Tax Credit

www.irs.gov (type "Child and Dependent Care Expenses" in the Search box)

You may be able to claim a tax credit if you are using child care or a child care program for your baby while you are working. Visit the website for further details and eligibility requirements, as well as to download the required forms necessary to apply for this benefit.

❧ Child Tax Credit (CTC)
www.irs.gov/formspubs (type "Child Tax Credit Forms" in the
    Search box)

Uncle Sam grants a tax credit to eligible families for each child under the age of seventeen. The credit will be increased from $600 to $1,000 per child by tax year 2010. The CTC is partially refundable for families with yearly earnings over $10,000. Visit the website for more information, as well as to download the CTC forms.

❧ Child Welfare League of America
In the United States, call 202-638-2952 (sorry, not a toll-free
    number)
www.cwla.org

The Child Welfare League of America assists more than 3.5 million abused and neglected children and their families each year. The organization offers families a wide range of services. For more information on the services available, call or check out the website for details.

❧ Early Head Start National Resource Center
U.S. Department of Health and Human Services
Head Start Bureau
330 C Street SW
Washington, DC 20202
In the United States, call 866-763-6481
www.ehsnrc.org

Early Head Start, a program for low-income families, provides services to low-income pregnant women, as well as families with infants and toddlers. This community-based program is designed to enhance children's physical, social, emotional, and intellectual development. It offers health, mental health, and family support services, including services to women before, during, and after pregnancy, information on nutrition, child care services, parenting education, and more. This program also supports parents by helping them move toward economic independence through various educational services. To find out if you are eligible to participate in this program, log on to the website or submit your questions about Early Head Start to the address listed above. This program is available to residents of the United States.

❀ Family and Medical Leave

In the United States, call 866-487-9243

www.dol.gov/asp/programs/guide/fmla.htm (U.S. Department of Labor)

www.nationalpartnership.org (click on "FMLA Guide" in the "Quick Jump" window)

The Family and Medical Leave Act (FMLA), enforced by the U.S. Department of Labor, is designed to help working people fulfill both their work and family responsibilities. This act allows families to take unpaid time off to care for their loved ones (such as caring for a new baby or newly adopted child or a sick parent, spouse, or child) or to recover from their own serious illnesses, without putting their jobs at risk. The FMLA covers any pregnancy-related leave that is medically necessary, including childbirth and recovery. Both a wife and a husband can each take up to twelve weeks' leave when the baby comes. You must have worked for your employer for at least twelve months and for a minimum of 1,250 hours during the last year, and you must work for a company with more than fifty employees to be eligible to take up to twelve weeks a year of unpaid leave that is job secured.

Click on "FAQ" for frequently asked questions about the Family and Medical Leave Act, as well as eligibility requirements. You can download a free copy of the "Guide to the Family and Medical Leave Act," which will give you current information on the act and eligibility requirements, at www.nationalpartnership.org. For questions about the FMLA, contact the U.S. Department of Labor's Wage and Hour Division at the toll-free number listed earlier, or contact your state labor department or your union.

✿ Federal Information Center
In the United States, call 800-FED-INFO

The National Call Center will answer your questions about federal agencies, programs, benefits, and services. Frequently requested information is given in recordings available through an automated service.

✿ Food Stamp Program
In the United States, call 800-221-5689 (USDA Food Stamp
    Information Line)
www.fns.usda.gov/fsp

In the fiscal year 2000, the Food Stamp Program helped put food on the table for 7.3 million households and 17.2 million individuals each day. The Food Stamp Program is a nutrition assistance program that provides low-income households with coupons they can use like cash at most grocery stores. The goal of this program is to ensure that families have access to a healthy diet. Food stamps can be used to buy many different food items, including baby food and cereal, bread, cheese and dairy products, and other food items for your baby and the whole family.

The Food Stamp Program is administered by the U.S. Department of Agriculture at the federal level, through its Food and Nutrition Service. You can go to a local food stamp office to fill out an application or call the office and ask for an application to be sent to you. For more information about the Food Stamp Program and eligibility requirements, contact the U.S. Department of Agriculture at 800-221-5689. Go online for further details. The eligibility requirements to receive food stamps are posted at www.foodusa.org.

❧ GovSpot.com

www.govspot.com

To help simplify the search for the best government resources and information online, the GovSpot is a guide to government information on the Web, a free source that offers a vast collection of top government and civic resources. Visit the website to locate federal agencies, use government search engines, find out what government benefits you're eligible for, and apply for financial aid. You can also get information on food and nutrition services, such as eligibility rules for food stamps; welfare information; and assistance with jobs, health, shelter, and housing. This free resource is available to residents of the United States only.

❧ SCHIP (State Children's Health Insurance Program)

In the United States, call 410-786-3000 (sorry, not a toll-free number)

www.policyalmanac.org/health/chip.shtml

The purpose of the SCHIP program is to provide free or low-cost health insurance to uninsured, low-income children. All uninsured children who are ineligible for Medicaid are eligible for SCHIP. Go to www.hcfa.gov/medicaid (click on "State Programs") for a listing of state SCHIP toll-free numbers. For more information, go online or call

❧ State Infertility Insurance Laws

www.asrm.org/Patients/insur.html

Visit this website to find out if your state mandates insurance coverage for fertility procedures, or to view an updated list of states and their laws.

❧ WIC (Women, Infants, and Children)

In the United States, call 703-305-2746 (sorry, not a toll-free number)

www.fns.usda.gov/wic

WIC is a government assistance program that offers outstanding assistance to eligible low-income families. This program serves 45 percent of all infants born in the United States. In fact, one in four new mothers participates in WIC. This program is available to low-income families and those who are nutritionally at risk. WIC will provide, free of charge, nutritious foods (such as infant formula, milk, bread, cheese, and cereal during your baby's first years) to needy families. WIC also provides free information on healthy eating and nutrition, breast-feeding, and education, as well as screening and referrals to other health, welfare, and social services. The program targets pregnant women (through pregnancy and up to six weeks after birth or after pregnancy ends), breast-feeding women (up to infant's first birthday), non–breast-feeding postpartum women, infants (up to the first birthday), and children up to their fifth birthday.

WIC operates through two thousand local agencies in ten thousand clinic sites, in fifty state health departments, in thirty-two Indian Tribal Organizations, and in American Samoa, the District of Columbia, Puerto Rico, Guam, and the Virgin Islands. Services are provided at hospitals, community centers, public housing sites, and schools across the United States. The toll-free numbers and addresses for each state are listed on WIC's website. Click on "State Contacts" to locate the contact information for your state, as well as to view the state's income eligibility guidelines. You can also call the number listed above to be directed to a WIC program in your state.

Free Financial Assistance, Tax Breaks, and Other Benefits in Canada

The Government of Canada offers tax benefits and financial assistance to families to help with the cost of raising children, as well as provides educational counseling and support services for those in need. Check out the following listings for more information on these various programs, services, and entitlements and their eligibility requirements.

❦ Canada Child Tax Benefit

In Canada, call 800-387-1193
www.ccra.gc.ca/benefits

The Canada Child Tax Benefit (CCTB) is a nontaxable payment to help families with the cost of raising children. It is paid monthly to eligible families with children under age eighteen. The CCTB also includes the National Child Benefit Supplement (NCBS), which is a monthly benefit for low-income families with children.

For more information about these benefits, call for a free copy of the pamphlet *Your Canada Child Tax Benefit*, or download a copy at the website.

❦ Canada Prenatal Nutrition Program

Health Canada
Finance Building
Tunney's Pasture
Ottawa, ON K1A 1B5
In Canada, call 613-952-0240 (sorry, not a toll-free number)
www.phac-aspc.gc.ca/dca-dea/programs-mes/cpnp_main_e.html

The Canada Prenatal Nutrition Program helps community organizations provide services to at-risk pregnant women, such as help with nutrition and breast-feeding, infant development, substance abuse problems, stress, and family violence. A variety of services are offered to improve birth outcomes with at-risk women, such as nutritional counseling, food supplements, education, referrals, and counseling on lifestyle issues. You can find more information about this program at the website or by contacting the Canada Prenatal Nutrition Program. For a complete listing of CPNP projects across Canada, visit the website and click on "Projects Directory Online."

❦ Canada Site

In Canada, call 800-O-CANADA
www.canada.gc.ca

For current information about Government of Canada services, call or visit the website.

❀ Disability Tax Credit

In Canada, call 800-959-8281

www.ccra.gc.ca/disability

The Disability Tax Credit is a nonrefundable tax credit for people who have a severe and prolonged mental or physical impairment. It is available to persons who support a child with a disability. For more information about the Disability Tax Credit, as well as eligibility requirements, call or visit the website.

❀ Easter Seal Society Financial Assistance Program

In Ontario, call 866-630-3336

www.easterseals.org/services/default.asp?load=direct

The Easter Seal Society offers financial assistance programs to families, children, and young adults with physical disabilities in Ontario. The society will assist with the cost of medical equipment purchases and rentals, as well as eligible services. Families must apply for registration to receive financial assistance from the Easter Seal Society. See the website or call for more details.

❀ Employment Insurance (EI) and Maternity, Parental and Sickness Benefits

In Canada, call 800-O-CANADA

www.hrsdc.gc.ca/en/ei/types/special.shtml

Parents with a child born or placed in their care for adoption on or after December 31, 2000, may be eligible for increased parental benefits, including Employment Insurance, Maternity, and Parental Benefits for up to a year. The Government of Canada has also reduced the number of accumulated hours of insured employment necessary to qualify for these benefits from seven hundred hours to six hundred hours.

The free pamphlet *Employment Insurance: New Maternity, Parental and Sickness Benefits* will answer your questions regarding maternity leave and parental benefits in Canada. Some of the topics covered are how to apply for benefits, who is eligible, the qualifying period, what information is needed to apply, and how long you can receive maternity benefits. Log on to the website for more information.

❧ Federal Child Support Guidelines
www.canada.justice.gc.ca (click on "Programs and Services," then "Child Support")

The Federal Child Support Guidelines set out the basic amount that parents providing child support should pay based on income, the number of children involved, and the province or territory where the parents live. For more information about these guidelines, visit the website.

❧ Nobody's Perfect
In Canada, call 613-237-7667 (sorry, not a toll-free number)
www.hc-sc.gc.ca (click on "Just for You," then "Parents," then "Nobody's Perfect")

Parents of children from birth to age five, who are young, single, or living in social, cultural, or geographic isolation or on a low income, as well as parents for whom parenting programs are not generally accessible, can receive support and education through the Nobody's Perfect Program. This program is offered as a series of six to eight weekly group sessions. For more information about this program, call your local public health department or community health center, or call the Canadian Association of Family Resource Programs at the above-listed number for further details. You can also check out the website for more details on this program.

❧ Ontario Child Care Supplement for Working Families
In Ontario, call
English: 800-263-7965 (Ministry of Finance)
French: 800-668-5821 (Ministry of Finance)

Qualifying families in Ontario are entitled to a monthly child care supplement from the government, according to their net family income. These supplements are tax-free and do not have to be reported on your tax return. For more information on how you can receive this additional child care benefit from the government, call the Ministry of Finance's Information Centre.

❀ Services for Children: Guide to Government of Canada Services for Children and Their Families
In Canada, call 800-O-CANADA
www.cio-bic.gc.ca/children-enfants/form_e.htm
www.communication.gc.ca/guides/children_enfants/index_e.html

This free guide lists the many services that the Government of Canada offers to parents and caregivers and explains how to get more information on these services. It is an excellent resource, providing information on such topics as child health, safety, and nutrition; tax measures and benefits to help with the costs of raising children; services for children or families with special needs; and educational resources. To order this free guide, fill out the online form or call.

❀ Tax Information Phone Services (TIPS)
In Canada, call 800-267-6999

This is a toll-free number that Canadians can call to help them determine whether or not they are eligible for the Canada Child Tax Benefit.

Additional Tax Measures and Benefits
In Canada, call 800-959-2221
www.cio-bic.gc.ca/children-enfants/02_e.htm

The following are other tax measures offered by the Government of Canada to help Canadian families with children:

- **Child Care Expenses.** You may be eligible to claim child care expenses on your tax return if you or your spouse or common-law partner paid for someone to care for your child so you could earn income from employment or self-employment, go to school, or do research during the year.

- **Equivalent-to-Spouse Amount.** You may be able to claim an equivalent-to-spouse amount on your tax return if you are single, divorced, separated, or widowed and support a child.

To find out more about these and other tax measures offered by the Government of Canada to help families with children, visit the website or call. To receive forms to apply for any of these benefits, call. You can also visit www.cra-arc.gc.ca/formspubs/menu-e.html to obtain the required forms to apply for these benefits.

Parenting Support Groups

When my first daughter, Kayla, was born, I can't tell you all the times I was up in the middle of the night, simply checking to make sure that she was breathing and lying safely on her back. I worried about every little cough, sneeze, and sniffle. I kept wondering, "Is my baby's condition normal? Is there something I should be doing?"

At times, I felt that my concerns were silly, that I was simply being an overprotective mom. But there were many times that I really could have used someone to talk to about my concerns.

After calling some of the following parenting support groups and other organizations, I was relieved to find out that my concerns weren't silly at all, and that, in fact, many new moms were experiencing the same concerns I had.

As a new parent, you are bound to be unsure of yourself and of what is best for your baby at times. Maybe you are having problems breast-feeding and can't get him to latch on properly, or maybe your baby is crying uncontrollably and you are wondering if she might have colic and what you can do to help, or maybe your baby has a fever and you are unsure of the medication to administer.

It's completely natural for a new parent to worry about these things. I can't name a single parent who hasn't. That's one of the reasons that I felt it necessary to compile a list of parenting support groups and organizations for you to call, to give you someone to talk to when you have a parenting question or concern. Most calls are free of charge, and many of these support groups and organizations are available 24/7.

For parents who don't know where to turn when a problem arises, the numbers listed in this chapter will put you in touch with trained professionals, including social workers and nurses, and parenting support group workers who can help you find the answers you are looking for. These professionals will address such concerns as breast-feeding, colic, SIDS, alcohol and drug abuse, AIDS, Down syndrome, premature births, adoption, family planning, and nutrition. Many of these groups and organizations also offer free programs and services, as well as free informational literature.

So in the middle of the night, even if you just need someone to talk to, remember that you are not alone. If you have a concern, no matter how small, give one of these groups a call. That's what they're there for. The staff at these groups or organizations are more than willing to help. And remember, there is no such thing as a stupid question. Call your doctor or get the help and support you need through these services.

As each situation is unique, the information provided by these support groups and organizations and their staff should not be used as a substitute for the medical care and personal attention of your physician or for any emergency situations.

AAMR
In the United States or Canada, call 800-424-3688
www.aamr.org

AAMR promotes universal human rights for people with intellectual disabilities and provides help and support to families. Call for information and free educational literature.

Americans with Disabilities Act
In the United States, call 800-514-0301

The U.S. Department of Justice provides information and free publications about the Americans with Disabilities Act (ADA) through the toll-free ADA Information Line. Specialists will provide general information about ADA, answer specific technical questions, or provide information about filing a complaint.

America's Pregnancy Helpline
In the United States or Canada, call 888-672-2296
www.americanpregnancy.org

Call to receive free and confidential information about your pregnancy, as well as sexual health–related issues. Pregnancy counselors will be happy to assist you on the following topics:

- Pregnancy wellness
- Women's health
- Contraception
- Fertility
- Infertility
- Parenting
- Unplanned pregnancy
- Legal concerns
- Pregnancy loss
- Your baby's first year

The toll-free number will also link you to support groups and child care assistance programs. You can also visit the website for a wealth of pregnancy-related articles, as well as an online discussion forum where you can talk with other expecting mothers.

Association for Children for Enforcement of Support
In the United States, call 800-537-7072
www.childsupport-aces.org/home.html

Association for Children for Enforcement of Support (ACES), a nonprofit child support organization consisting of concerned parents whose children are entitled to support, is dedicated to improving child support enforcement. ACES provides the free self-help handbook *How to Collect Child Support*, which includes information regarding collecting child support, visitation problems, child support laws, government agencies, and enforcement methods for collecting child support payments. There is a small membership fee (based on your income) to join ACES. However, ACES will waive dues for special circumstances. Go online or call for further details.

❧ Birthright International (Pregnancy & Young Hotline)

In the United States or Canada, call 800-550-4900
www.birthright.org

If you're young, pregnant, and in need of help, Birthright International can help. Birthright International, an international pregnancy crisis center, will help you in making a decision about your pregnancy. They offer free pregnancy tests, one-on-one contact with personal, confidential counseling, maternity and baby clothes, housing referrals, adoption information, and more. These services are available to residents of the United States and Canada.

❧ Canada Pregnancy Hotline

In Canada, call 800-665-0570

Call the pregnancy hotline to find answers to your pregnancy questions, including breast-feeding, abortion, and other areas of concern. When you call this number, they will help to connect and refer you to the closest crisis pregnancy center in your area.

❧ Child Find of America, Inc.

In the United States or Canada, call 800-426-5678
www.childfindofamerica.org

Child Find of America is a not-for-profit charity whose mission is to locate missing children and prevent child abduction. In the unfortunate event that your child goes missing, contact Child Find for assistance.

❦ Children and Adults with Attention-Deficit/ Hyperactivity Disorder
In the United States or Canada, call 800-233-4050
www.chadd.org

Children and Adults with Attention-Deficit/Hyperactivity Disorder offers education, advocacy, and support for children and adults with ADHD. The website provides information and resources about ADHD.

❦ Council for Exceptional Children
In the United States, call 866-915-5000
www.cec.sped.org

The Council for Exceptional Children is available for persons concerned with the education of exceptional children. The organization provides educational, informational, and support services for handicapped and gifted children.

❦ Danny Foundation
In the United States, call 800-83-DANNY
www.dannyfoundation.org

The primary focus of the Danny Foundation is to help prevent unintentional injuries by educating the public about crib dangers, as well as to set standards for safe nursery products. To be sure that your crib is safe for your baby and meets the current safety standards, check out the Crib Safety Checklist at the website. Call to receive a checklist and recall information by mail. This offer is available to residents of the United States only.

❦ Easter Seals
In the United States, call 800-221-6827
www.easterseals.com

Easter Seals offers help and support to children and adults with disabilities. Services include helping children with disabilities succeed in school, helping people learn job skills and enter the workplace, providing rehabilitation services, as well as various other assistance programs. The children's services include infant monitoring programs to recognize developmental delays and help parents measure an infant's skills; affordable, high-quality child care; and help for infants born into substance-abusing families and to teenage mothers. For more details, visit the website or call.

✿ Endometriosis Association
In the United States, call 800-992-3636
In Canada, call 800-426-2END
www.endometriosisassn.org

The Endometriosis Association is an organization that offers help, support, and pertinent medical information to women with endometriosis. Call to find out about the free endometriosis-screening program, as well as to receive general information about endometriosis.

✿ Family and Home Network
www.familyandhome.org

The Family and Home website is a support site for parents staying home to raise their children. Their site provides support and encouragement to mothers and fathers across the United States and around the world. The "member-only" area provides parents with opportunities to connect with other members.

✿ Family Service Canada
In Canada, call 800-668-7808
www.familyservicecanada.org

The mission of Family Service Canada is "to promote families as the primary source of nurture and development of individuals, to promote quality services which strengthen families and communities, and to advocate policies and legislation which advance family well-being in Canada." The organization provides a wide range of services, programs, and resources for families and individuals in Canada.

❧ First Candle/SIDS Alliance

In the United States, call 800-221-7437

The SIDS Alliance provides information on sudden infant death syndrome and explains the correct sleeping positions for infants, as well as other important facts that you need to know to reduce the risk of SIDS and suffocation. Call for further information on SIDS, as well as to request free SIDS literature.

❧ Gerber Parents Resource Center

In the United States or Canada, call 800-4-GERBER

Call the Gerber Parents Resource Center with all of your baby care or feeding questions. A certified lactation educator is available 24/7 to answer your questions.

❧ Harbor House

www.harbor-house.org

Harbor House is a nonprofit organization dedicated to the recovery of single mothers with chemical dependencies. Harbor House provides a home for these women with a caring, structured, and disciplined environment. They offer several programs, including life skills, job training, and education, available to residents of Toledo, Ohio.

❧ INCIID (InterNational Council on Infertility Information Dissemination)

www.inciid.org/index.php

INCIID (pronounced "inside") is a nonprofit organization that provides information and support regarding the diagnosis, treatment, and prevention of infertility and miscarriage and pregnancy loss. They offer guidance to those considering adoption or child-free lifestyles.

❦ Jesse Cause Foundation

In the United States or Canada, call 805-984-7933 (sorry, not a toll-free number)

www.thejessecause.org

Group B Strep is the number one infectious killer of newborn infants in the United States. Some babies have died within days or weeks of birth; others have suffered terrifying brain surgeries, loss of sight and hearing, as well as reduced mental or physical aptitude, according to the Jesse Cause Foundation. The Centers for Disease Control and Prevention states that close to 90 percent of these tragedies can be prevented by giving pregnant women a noninvasive test and treating them with antibiotics during labor. As many people haven't heard of Group B Strep, and as some doctors are still not routinely screening or educating women about the risk of Group B Strep, the Jesse Cause Foundation places emphasis on universally testing every pregnant woman and raising public awareness about this infectious killer. Call or visit the website for more information.

❦ Johnson & Johnson Pediatric Institute, L.L.C.

In the United States, call 877-JNJ-LINK

In Canada, call 631-208-9238 (sorry, not a toll-free number)

www.jjpi.com

One phone call to the Johnson & Johnson Pediatric Institute will give you the most up-to-date information on today's parenting topics from the expertise of thousands of specialists from around the world. The organization offers a variety of easy-to-understand booklets and videos on child development and parenting.

❦ La Leche League Canada

In Canada, call 800-665-4324

www.lalecheleaguecanada.ca

The La Leche League is a priceless resource for moms who breast-feed. The organization offers up-to-date information on breast-feeding, such as how to know when your baby is getting enough milk, how to know when it is time for a feeding, what types of food a breast-feeding mother should eat, and how to store expressed breast milk. Call for references and referrals in your area or visit the website for current breast-feeding information.

❧ La Leche League International (U.S.)
In the United States, call 800-LALECHE
www.lalecheleague.org

The La Leche League is the only organization with the sole purpose of helping moms who breast-feed. The organization has some three thousand local groups in the United States, which meet regularly to share breast-feeding information and mothering experience. It is a priceless resource for all moms who breast-feed. You can get up-to-date information on breast-feeding; for example, the correct positioning of the baby at the breast, how to know when your baby is getting enough milk, how to know when it is time for a feeding, what types of food a breast-feeding mother should eat, and how to store expressed breast milk. Call to receive telephone counseling, as well as to receive references and referrals in your area. Visit the website for current breast-feeding information.

❧ Make-a-Wish Foundation
In the United States, call 800-722-WISH
In Canada, call 888-822-WISH
U.S. website: www.wish.org
Canadian website: www.makeawish.ca

The goal of the Make-a-Wish Foundation is to grant the wishes of children with life-threatening illnesses. If you know a child with a life-threatening illness, please call the Make-a-Wish Foundation.

❀ **March of Dimes**
>   In the United States or Canada, call 888-MODIMES
>   www.modimes.org

The March of Dimes Pregnancy and Newborn Health Education Center is a great place to call when you're expecting. Pregnancy information experts will answer your questions on pregnancy, birth defects, and more. You can also call to receive a special packet of materials for parents and families who have experienced the loss of a child between conception and the first month of life.

❀ **Motherisk**
>   www.motherisk.org

Motherisk is available to provide information and guidance to pregnant or lactating moms regarding the safety or risk of drugs, chemicals, diseases, infections, and other exposures during pregnancy.

• **Alcohol and Substance Use in Pregnancy Helpline.** In the United States, call 416-813-8738 (sorry, not a toll-free number). In Canada, call 877-FAS-INFO. This help line will provide pregnant and breast-feeding women and their families with information on alcohol and substance use in pregnancy, including the possible effects of alcohol and other substances on their baby.

• **General Exposures in Pregnancy and Breast-feeding.** In the United States or Canada, call 416-813-6780 (sorry, not a toll-free number). It is probably still safe for you to breast-feed your baby even if you are taking medication. If you are unsure about the effect of a medication on breast-feeding or pregnancy, call Motherisk for information.

• **HIV Healthline and Network.** In the United States or Canada, call 888-246-5840. Call to receive confidential counseling about the risk of HIV and about HIV treatment in pregnancy, as well as for access to information and care for women on issues involved in HIV infections during pregnancy and breast-feeding.

• **Nausea and Vomiting in Pregnancy Helpline.** In the United States or Canada, call 800-436-8477. According to Motherisk, nausea and vomiting in pregnancy (NVP), also referred to as "morning sickness," is very common, afflicting up to 80 percent of pregnant women. Call for support and information about morning sickness, including its effects, ways to help alleviate morning sickness, and answers about care and treatment.

National Adoption Center
In the United States, call 800-862-3678
www.adopt.org

The National Adoption Center works with social workers and other adoption professionals to bring children and families together throughout the United States. Adoption professionals list available children and interested families and make matches between them. If you have completed a home study and are approved to adopt, you can register on the National Adoption Exchange. The center also offers information and referral services, and it provides resource materials and adoption information packages on a variety of topics. Call for further information.

National Dissemination Center for Children with Disabilities (NICHCY)
In the United States, call 800-695-0285
www.nichcy.org

NICHCY is a national information and referral center. It provides information on disabilities and disability-related issues for families, with a special focus on children and youth from birth to twenty-two years of age. You can call to speak to an information specialist, as well as to receive publications and fact sheets on specific disabilities, resource sheets, parent guides, and more.

National Down Syndrome Society Hotline
In the United States or Canada, call 800-221-4602
www.ndss.org

The National Down Syndrome Society has a toll-free help line that parents can call to get general information about Down syndrome, as well as referrals to local parent support groups. New parents can call and request a free new parent packet.

❦ National Life Center (Pregnancy Hotline)
In the United States or Canada, call 800-848-LOVE
www.nationallifecenter.com

With access to over 3,500 pregnancy centers across the United States, the National Life Center offers free guidance and counseling to women facing pregnancy. Their organization has helped save half a million babies. They offer anonymous pregnancy testing and will help you find medical, legal, or psychological help; shelter; public assistance; housing; education and occupation guidance; maternity and baby clothes; formula; and adoption referral as desired. Their free services are completely confidential.

❦ Nurturing Network
In the United States or Canada, call 800-TNN-4MOM
www.nurturingnetwork.org

The Nurturing Network is an international charitable organization with more than thirty-two thousand volunteer members who have provided for the immediate practical needs of nearly fifteen thousand women facing the crisis of an unplanned pregnancy. The Nurturing Network offers individually tailored, life-saving resources to women whose own support networks have let them down, with special emphasis on assisting college and working women. This comprehensive support includes professional counseling, medical services, residential assistance, and educational, employment, and financial resources. The network invites clients and volunteers in the United States and Canada who either need help or can offer help to call for further information.

☙ **Option Line (National Pregnancy Helpline)**
In the United States or Canada, call 800-395-HELP
E-mail: answers@optionline.org
www.pregnancycenters.org

Call, or e-mail Option Line to talk to a trained pregnancy counselor who will help answer all of your pregnancy-related questions and refer you to the pregnancy center nearest you. These pregnancy centers offer free pregnancy tests, peer counseling, post-abortion help, and information about pregnancy symptoms, fetal development, abortion procedures, abortion risks, and more. Visit the website to view a listing of toll-free pregnancy help hotlines and pregnancy care centers in the United States and Canada.

☙ **Our Missing Children**
In the United States or Canada, call 877-318-3576
www.ourmissingchildren.ca

Our Missing Children, a program created by the Government of Canada, provides assistance to parents when their children are missing. Resources include a photo-aging service, investigative assistance, and international networking.

☙ **Parent Help Line**
In Canada, call 888-603-9100
www.parentsinfo.sympatico.ca

The Parent Help Line is Canada's first national, bilingual toll-free phone counseling and referral service for parents and caregivers. It gives parents a place to turn for any parenting concerns, 24/7. Leading experts developed it to give guidance, information, and support to parents of children from birth to age nineteen. When you call, you will receive confidential counseling from professionally trained counselors. The Parent Help Line also provides you with a library of recorded messages on hundreds of parenting issues.

❧ Parents Without Partners

In the United States or Canada, call 800-637-7974
www.parentswithoutpartners.org

Parents Without Partners is a resource for single parents and their children. The organization has chapters in both Canada and the United States and is the "largest international, nonprofit membership organization devoted to the welfare and interests of single parents and their children." Chapters run programs of educational activities, family activities, and adult social/recreational activities, which feature discussions, study groups, and professional speakers. Call or log on to the website to find a Parents Without Partners chapter in your area.

❧ Planned Parenthood

In the United States, call 800-230-PLAN
www.plannedparenthood.org

Planned Parenthood affiliate health centers provide affordable health care to nearly five million people every year. Call, or visit the Planned Parenthood website for sexual health information, for answers to medical questions, or to schedule an appointment at the Planned Parenthood center in your area. This service is available to residents of the United States only.

❧ Poison Control, Wherever You Are

In the United States, call 800-222-1222

Keep this number by your phone or posted on your fridge. When you dial this toll-free hotline, you'll automatically be connected to the closest poison control center. You can call this number 24/7 to talk to a poison expert or if you have a poison emergency. This toll-free number is available to residents of the United States only.

❧ Poison Information Centres

The following are hotlines to reach the various Poison Information Centres in Canada:

Alberta: 800-332-1414

British Columbia: 800-567-8911

Manitoba: 204-787-2591 (sorry, not a toll-free number)

New Brunswick: 506-857-5555 (sorry, not a toll-free number)

Newfoundland: 709-722-1110 (sorry, not a toll-free number)

Northwest Territories: 867-669-4100 (sorry, not a toll-free number)

Nova Scotia: 800-565-8161

Ontario: 800-268-9017

Quebec: 800-463-5060

Saskatchewan: 800-363-7474

Yukon: 867-667-8726 (sorry, not a toll-free number)

Ross Healthcare Hotline
In Canada, call 800-670-7878

The Ross Healthcare Hotline is available to answer your questions about feeding your baby. Call anytime to speak to a registered nurse.

RSV Hotline
In the United States or Canada, call 877-906-7085

A premature infant can be at an increased risk for serious RSV (respiratory syncytial virus) disease. For more information about RSV and what can be done to prevent it in premature infants, call the hotline.

Salvation Army
In the United States or Canada, call 800-SAL-ARMY
www.salvationarmy.org

If you are in need, this number will connect you to your local Salvation Army for information on current programs and services that are offered in the areas of volunteer services, day care referral, drug and alcohol counseling, emergency and disaster, prayer and counseling, missing persons, and more. You can also call this number to make a charitable donation or arrange for a thrift-store pickup.

❀ **SHARE Pregnancy & Infant Loss Support, Inc.**
In the United States, call 800-821-6819
www.nationalshareoffice.com

SHARE offers support for parents experiencing pregnancy and infant loss through early pregnancy loss, stillborn, or newborn death. Their services offer free information packets and resources and support to bereaved parents. They also offer telephone support to bereaved parents, friends, and family members; help in connecting parents with support groups in their area; an interactive website with a message board and chats; and more.

❀ **Spina Bifida Association of America**
In the United States or Canada, call 800-621-3141
www.sbaa.org

Spina bifida results from the failure of the spine to close properly during the first month of pregnancy. According to the Spina Bifida Association of America, it is the most frequently occurring birth defect, affecting approximately one out of every one thousand newborns in the United States. Having the goal of promoting the prevention of spina bifida, the Spina Bifida Association of America provides a toll-free number that offers information and referral service, as well as publications relating to spina bifida and information regarding the importance of folic acid in women trying to conceive.

❀ **Telehealth Ontario**
In Ontario, call 866-797-0000

At Telehealth Ontario, a registered nurse is available 24/7 to answer all of your health-related questions.

❀ **Transport Canada**
In Canada, call 800-333-0371

A forward-facing child seat is completely anchored only when the top strap is securely tethered to the vehicle. If you can't find your vehicle's tether anchorage, call Transport Canada for assistance, as well as to receive information on other motor vehicle and road safety issues.

❧ Triaminic Clinic

In the United States, call 800-KIDS-987

www.triaminicclinic.com

The Triaminic Clinic is a twenty-four-hour resource for information and helpful tips about your child's cold and allergy needs. Call, or visit the website for further information.

❧ Women Work! The National Network for Women's Employment

In the United States, call 800-235-2732

www.womenwork.org

Women Work! offers more than one thousand education, training, and employment programs to women across America. This program helps women find jobs to support their families and helps them to achieve economic self-sufficiency. Check out the website or call for further information or to request a resource pack containing referral information. This program is available to residents of the United States only.

Saving for Your Baby's Future

According to the Canadian Scholarship Trust Plan, it is estimated that in the year 2019, a four-year degree will cost $151,000 Canadian or $75,000 U.S.—ouch! Although it may seem like a long time away at this point, it is definitely a good idea to start saving as soon as possible for your child's education, spreading the payments out over several years.

There are many different types of savings programs available. Speak to a financial adviser to find the one that suits you and your family the best. Keep in mind that you don't need to invest a large amount of money—some of the programs available require only a minimal monthly investment.

❀ BabyMint
www.babymint.com

Parents who join the free BabyMint program can save for their child's future education every time they make purchases at hundreds of leading retailers. The BabyMint program is a free college savings program that allows parents to save up to $50,000 for their child's college tuition. With each purchase you make at a participating retailer, a cash-back contribution is earned and then automatically deposited into an education investment account set up for your child. Retailers' contributions can go as high as 20 percent of your total purchase and are automatically deposited into your account. Grandparents and other relatives of the family can also join and direct their BabyMint cash-back earnings to your child's savings account. Visit the BabyMint website to receive more details and to complete a membership application. This program is available to residents of the United States only.

Canada Education Savings Grant Program
In Canada, call 888-276-3624
www.hrdc-drhc.gc.ca (click on "Children," then "Canada Education Savings Grant")

More than 1.5 million Canadians have opened a Registered Education Savings Plan (RESP). With the Canada Education Savings Grant Program, you can start saving for your child's education now and receive an extra 20 percent contribution from the Government of Canada. Check online or call for details.

Gerber Life Grow-Up Plan
In the United States or Canada, call 800-311-2055
www.gerberlife.com

The Gerber Life Grow-Up Plan is designed to provide life insurance protection to children between fourteen days and twelve years of age. Call to receive a free Gerber Grow-Up Plan insurance information packet and application. This offer is available to residents of the United States and Canada.

Upromise
www.upromise.com

Upromise is a free college savings program. Thousands of companies participate in this program and will contribute a portion of what you spend with them to your Upromise account to help you save for college. Some of the participating companies include Toys "R" Us, Babies "R" Us, Kids "R" Us, Staples, Borders, Waldenbooks, Exxon, and Mobil, to name a few. You will also receive a college savings contribution when you buy particular grocery items at your local participating grocery store and when you dine at various restaurants, including McDonald's and more than seven thousand other restaurants, as well as when you shop online. Grandparents and friends can also contribute to your college savings account.

The website offers a Search box to help you find participating stores in your area. Go online for further details on how you can open up a free Upromise account. This savings program is available to residents of the United States only.

Mom's Free Stuff

Mom has had a hard day—to put it mildly! Baby decided to wear his cereal bowl as a hat at breakfast. When the mail carrier arrived at the front door with the mail at lunchtime, baby said his first word, "Dada." And while at the grocery store in the evening, baby pulled a tampon out of your purse at the checkout counter, waving it around like a baton!

A day in the life of a new mom isn't always easy. It seems like children are at their most exuberant when their parents are the most exhausted! There are bound to be pull-out-your-hair types of days when nothing seems to go right.

In the midst of all the chaos and endless diaper changes, sometimes it seems that we forget about ourselves. It is important for new moms to take care of themselves as much as possible and to take time out to recharge and reenergize.

Because you deserve a break now and then, I've included in this chapter some free items for you to pamper yourself with—some luxury bath products to help you unwind; free makeup, hair, and perfume samples; recipes; cool savings; plus a treasure trove of other terrific freebies I think you'll really enjoy!

Beauty Products to Pamper Mom

The following companies offer free beauty samples from time to time. Visit their websites or call their toll-free numbers. If offers are not available the first time around, check back frequently, as many of these companies will relist an offer at a future date or add an even newer promotional item for you to try out.

❀ Almay

www.almay.com/register.asp

Register online to get special notice about Almay's new products, contests, free samples, coupons, and more. This offer is available to residents of the United States and Canada.

❀ Apple a Day

www.appleaday.com (click on "Free Trial Samples")

Sign up to receive a free trial sample of the "New You" Skin Rejuvenation System, created to give you healthy, smooth, younger-looking skin. This offer is available to residents of the United States and Canada.

❀ Arbonne and Mertzlufft & Associates

www.mertzlufft.com (click on "Free Samples")

Fill out an online form to receive free samples of skin care products. This offer is available to residents of the United States and Canada.

❀ *Beauty Sense*

www.BeautySense.com

The *Beauty Sense* e-magazine is filled with great tips and free product offers for moms, as well as exclusive access to the *Beauty Sense* BeautySpa—a great place to relax and recharge. This offer is available to residents of the United States only.

❧ Beauty Tips Online
www.beautytipsonline.com/freebies.htm

Beauty Tips Online offers free tips and tricks on skin care, hair care, makeup, fitness, and more. Visit the website to sign up for free beauty samples, cosmetics, and contests.

❧ Club Med
www.clubmedbeauty.com

Log on to the Club Med website to receive a free sample of My Ocean fragrance or other current promotional offers. This offer is available to residents of the United States only.

❧ Coty Shop
www.cotyshop.com (click on "Coty Beauty Pass")

Visit the Coty Shop to request free samples of Coty products, to find out how you can enter their sweepstakes, to learn about new products, and more. This offer is available to residents of the United States and Canada.

❧ Cover Girl
www.covergirl.com

Log on to Cover Girl's website to enter contests, receive free makeup samples intermittently throughout the year, and more. This offer is available to residents of the United States and Canada.

❧ Dove
In the United States or Canada, call 800-598-5005
U.S. website: www.dove.com (click on "Join Your Dove")
Canadian website: www.dove.ca/contact/opt_in

For samples, offers, and previews from Dove or other Unilever brands, call the toll-free number or sign up online. This offer is available to residents of the United States and Canada.

❧ Dream Perfumes

www.dreamperfumes.com

Dream Perfumes is offering several free perfume samples for you to try:

- Bitch is "a new wild and seductive fragrance" from Gosh International. Order a free sample at www.houseofgosh .com/bitch.htm.
- K-A-O-S is a new fragrance from Gosh International "that will turn your world upside down." Order a free sample at www .houseofgosh.com/k-a-o-s.htm.
- Ottomane is a "warm and sensual fragrance" from Ulric de Varens. Order a free sample at www.houseofgosh.com/ ottomane.htm.
- Rue Pergolese is a fragrance from Ulric de Varens, named after a quaint side street in Paris. Order a free sample at www .houseofgosh.com/ruepergolese.htm.
- Varensia is a "fruity floral with a gently entrancing fragrance" from Ulric de Varens. Order a free sample at www.houseofgosh .com/varensia.htm.

These offers are available to residents of the United States only.

❧ Enchantress Hosiery

www.enchantresshosiery.com/free/default.asp

To introduce you to its fine line of hosiery, Enchantress will send you a free pair of pantyhose. Check out the website for details. This offer is available to residents of Canada only.

❧ Free-Beauty-Samples.Com

www.free-beauty-samples.com

Free-Beauty-Samples.Com will send you free makeup and a daily newsletter just for joining. This offer is available to residents of the United States only.

Freebies for Women
www.freebiesforwomen.com

The Freebies for Women website gives away free samples every day, including free soaps, lotions, cosmetics, and other gifts and prizes. Visit the website for details.

Free Cosmetics
www.1freebieaday.com/free_cosmetics.html

At this website you can receive cosmetics, beauty products, and fragrances absolutely free. Go online for details. This offer is good for residents of the United States only.

Head & Shoulders
www.headandshoulders.com/usa/free_samples

Complete an online questionnaire to receive a free sample of a new Head & Shoulders shampoo. This offer is available to residents of the United States only.

Herbal Essences
U.S. website: www.herbalessences.com/us/home.asp
Canadian website: www.herbalessences.com/club/ca-en/join.asp

Join Club Herbal to take advantage of special offers from Herbal Essences, including free product samples and sneak previews of new products. This offer is available to residents of the United States and Canada.

L'Oreal Paris Canada
www.lorealparis.ca

Register at L'Oreal Paris to join the "Beauty Lounge" and receive free VIP Beauty Lounge coupons, samples, beauty advice, and other special offers from L'Oreal. This offer is available to residents of Canada only.

❀ L'Oreal Paris USA

www.lorealparisusa.com (click on "Special Offers")

Visit the L'Oreal website to sign up for special offers from L'Oreal, including discount coupons, free samples, and more. This offer is available to residents of the United States only.

❀ Masada

www.masada-spa.com/feedback.html

All of Masada's spa products contain 100 percent natural, unprocessed mineral salts from the Dead Sea. For more information about this company, and to receive a free sample packet of one of their products, fill out the form at the Masada website. This offer is available to residents of the United States and Canada.

❀ Maybelline

www.maybelline.com

Maybelline offers free samples, sweepstakes, and other special offers from time to time. Visit the website to check out their current offers, or to sign up for their free newsletter. This offer is available to residents of the United States and Canada.

❀ Neutrogena

U.S. website: www.neutrogena.com (click on "My Neutrogena")
Canadian website: www.neutrogena.ca

The Neutrogena website offers free product samples and other promotional offers from time to time at their website. Visit the website to sign up for their current promotional offer.

❀ Olay

www.total-effects.com/sample/sample.shtml

This website offers free samples of Olay skincare products or other current promotional items. This offer is available to residents of the United States only.

❧ Pantene Pro-V

www.pantene.com (click on "Become a Pantene Insider")

When you become a "Pantene Insider," you'll receive free inside information from Pantene, personalized hair solutions, stylist advice, exclusive sweepstakes, other offers, and more. This offer is available to residents of the United States and Canada.

❧ Rembrandt Oral Care Products

In the United States, call 800-548-3663
www.rembrandt.com

Rembrandt offers free product samples and discount coupons for money off Rembrandt Oral Care Products periodically throughout the year. Call or go online to request a free sample or coupon. This offer is available to residents of the United States only.

❧ Revlon

www.revlon.com (click on "Register")

Register at the Revlon website to receive special notice about Revlon's new products, contests, free samples, coupons, and more. This offer is available to residents of the United States and Canada.

❧ Sonya Dakar

www.sonyadakar.com/shared/skin-chart.htm

Sonya Dakar offers online visitors a complimentary skin consultation and a free gift by mail. Visit the website for more details. This offer is available to residents of the United States only.

❦ Uncle Harry's Natural Products

www.uncleharrys.com (click on "Sample Request")

Uncle Harry's Natural Tooth Powder is made of 100 percent natural ingredients. Fill out the online form to receive a free sample. This offer is available to residents of the United States and Canada.

❦ Unilever

In Canada, call 800-598-5005

Call to receive a free Caress Silkening Body Lotion sample or another free promotional item from Unilever. This offer is available to residents of Canada only.

❦ Women Freebies

www.womenfreebies.com

This site offers loads of free stuff for moms, including free beauty and cosmetic samples, health samples, sweepstakes, and more.

Free Recipes and Recipe Books

Why go out and buy expensive cookbooks when you can get tons of fabulous recipes and recipe books for free! The following companies offer lots of great recipe ideas that your whole family will enjoy.

❦ Allrecipes

www.allrecipes.com

The Allrecipes website presents an assortment of great recipes, meal ideas, and cooking advice. Categories in the recipe collection include appetizers, brunch, quick and easy meals, desserts, holiday cooking, and more.

❦ Canned Food Alliance

www.mealtime.org

The Canned Food Alliance recipe database contains hundreds of healthy recipes, complete with preparation time, cooking time, and nutritional information.

🎀 Dare Foods

www.15minutestofame.com/recipes.htm

This website features some great recipes from Dare Foods. These recipes take fifteen minutes or less to prepare.

🎀 Domino Sugar

www.dominosugar.com

The Domino Sugar website is filled with wonderful recipes and great fun for you and your kids. There are many ideas for delicious meals and snacks for your family, such as dips and spreads, appetizers, salads, and desserts.

🎀 Eden Foods

www.edenfoods.com

Eden Foods, a natural and organic food company, lists more than four hundred recipes on its website. You can search for recipes by type of meal, culture of origin, or recipe contents.

🎀 FamilyTime

www.familytime.com

At this website you will find great ideas for recipes, meals, entertaining, and family fun. Of the more than four thousand recipes are some from Campbell's, McCormick, Nestlé, and Swanson, as well as recipes listed by region, including Asian, Italian, Mediterranean, and others.

🎀 Fresh Del Monte Produce Inc.

www.freshdelmonte.com (click on "Kid Zone," then "Free Stuff")

At this website you can download the *Del Monte Hawaii Gold Pineapple Cookbook* for free.

❦ Hidden Valley
In the United States, call 800-537-2823

Call to receive a free recipe collection from Hidden Valley. This offer is available to residents of the United States only.

❦ Kraft Foods
U.S. website: www.kraftfoods.com (click on "Get Recipes")
Canadian website: www.kraftcanada.com

At the Kraft Foods website you can search for recipes by recipe title, ingredients, meal occasion, or recipe type. Click on "Promotions" to enter their latest sweepstakes.

❦ Land O'Lakes
www.landolakes.com

Hundreds of free recipes, meal ideas, and baking tips are available at the Land O'Lakes website in several different categories, such as "Appetizers," "Side Dishes," "Bread," and "Cakes."

❦ M&M's
In the United States, call 800-627-7852
In Canada, call 888-709-6277
www.m-ms.com/us/baking

Call for a free M&M's recipe book. You can also check out the M&M's website for yummy M&M's recipes your kids will love, including cakes, brownies and bars, ice cream, delicious cookies, and other sweet treats. This offer is available to residents of the United States and Canada.

❀ Reynolds Kitchens

www.reynoldskitchen.com (click on "Order Brochures")

Reynolds Kitchens offers free brochures with great tips, hints, and ideas. Fill out the online form to receive a selection of brochures. Tons of delicious free recipes are also available for you to view at this website, with topics including "Cooking for Company," "Delicious Desserts," "On the Grill," and more. This offer is available to residents of the United States and Canada.

❀ Sunsweet

In the United States, call 800-417-2253

Call to receive free recipes from Sunsweet. This offer is available to residents of the United States only.

❀ Swanson

www.swansonbroth.com/cookbook_offer.asp

The free Swanson Broth cookbook *Creative Cooking* contains thirty new recipes, a special holiday section, and more. You can order this free cookbook online. This offer is available to residents of the United States only.

For the Craftsy Parent

Crafts and hobbies can be a great way for parents to unwind and relieve stress, and they allow you to explore your creative side and try something new. The following websites offer free craft projects and craft sheets that you can print out from your computer. If you're great at sewing, there are even some online patterns you can use to make your own baby clothing and accessories.

❧ 1 Stop Free Shop

www.1stopfreeshop.com/craftpatterns.htm

There are hundreds of free craft patterns to choose from at this website, such as birdhouse patterns, candle patterns, folk art patterns, floral patterns, paints and painting patterns, and more. Photos, materials needed, and complete instructions are also included.

❧ AllCrafts

www.allcrafts.net

This terrific site is a crafter's dream come true. At AllCrafts you will find hundreds of free craft projects in many different categories, such as holiday crafts, kids' crafts, nature crafts, candle- and soap-making crafts, rubber-stamping, and scrapbooking. You will also find a wealth of free craft patterns that you can print out.

❧ Ben Franklin

www.benfranklinstores.com (click on "Projects")

The Ben Franklin website has an assortment of free craft project sheets that you can print out. The supplies that you will need are listed, and the instructions to complete these craft projects are given.

❧ Cloth Doll Connection

www.clothdollconnection.com/FreePatterns.html

At the Cloth Doll Connection you can print out free cloth doll patterns. There are several different patterns to choose from. Instructions and supplies needed to complete these projects are also featured.

❧ Craftown

www.craftown.com

The craftsy mom will find everything she needs at this terrific website, which features country, Victorian, and holiday crafts; instructions for candle and jewelry making; and free craft patterns for crochet, knitting, quilting, kids' crafts, and more. The website also offers free online tutorials where you can learn a new crafts skill at the learning center.

Free Craftz Patternz
www.freecraftz.com

This excellent crafter's website offers numerous free craft patterns, including online tole painting patterns, folk art patterns, and woodworking projects, as well as adorable country angel and Raggedy Annie patterns that you can simply print out. Links to other crafting websites are provided as well.

Martingale & Company
www2.martingale-pub.com/freepatterns/default.htm

This crafts website offers free printable patterns and instructions for quilters, knitters, and crafters.

Sue's CrochetandKnitting.com
www.crochetandknitting.com/patterns.htm

Visit this website to print out patterns to make crocheted baby socks and slippers for your infant.

Just for Fun!

Head over to the Virtual Chocolate website to check out the mouthwatering selection of delicious, heavenly chocolates. Then surf over to the Virtual Presents website where you can dream the day away, imagining owning a brand new Porsche or taking an exotic vacation. You can even send these virtual presents as postcards to someone special!

You'll find some really fun and tasty websites in this section. Grab a cup of tea or coffee, sit down, and check out these websites—just for fun!

✿ 2CoolBaby

www.2coolbaby.com/12ROSES.htm

This website offers printable coupons aimed at busy parents who have very few intimate moments together. There are twelve romantic coupons to choose from, including "Full Body Massage," "Breakfast in Bed (served wearing only a smile)," and "Candlelit Bubble Bath." Take time out to enjoy these coupons with your spouse!

✿ AmericanGreetings.com

www.americangreetings.com

AmericanGreetings.com offers a terrific selection of free online greetings in such areas as friendship, recipes, and love and dating. Also available is a huge selection of really cool music greetings, courtesy of BeatGreets, with more than three hundred artists to choose from! Many of the greetings at this website are animated. You can include a personal message on your greeting and send it via e-mail to someone special. And if you'd rather send a card by snail mail, click on "Free Coupon" for a coupon you can print out and redeem at participating retailers.

✿ Freebies for Women

www.freebiesforwomen.com/notepads.shtml

The Freebies for Women website features several free notepads for you to print out and use. Some of these notepads are for grocery shopping lists and errands, others are just for doodling. You can print out as many of these funny and original notepads as you like.

✿ Mom's Break Village

www.momsbreak.com (click on "Iron-On Transfers")

The Mom's Break website offers a large assortment of free iron-on transfers that you can print out on transfer paper. Some of the cute sayings for your transfers are as follows: "Yes, I Am Pregnant!," "Mommy To Be," "Grandmas Give the Best Hugs," and "Grandpas Give the Best Hugs." At this website you will also find free baby shower games, baby announcements, and baby shower, pregnancy, and kids' birthday printables, including invitations, iron-on transfers, and more.

❧ Original Country Clipart by Lisa
www.countryclipart.com/recipecards.htm

This website offers some cute country recipe cards, shopping lists, gift tags, and to-do lists that you can print out for free.

❧ Virtual Chocolate
www.virtualchocolate.com

Chocolate lovers will definitely love this website! You can send luscious and heavenly virtual chocolate treats, chocolate electronic postcards, and more to a favorite friend in cyberspace. So much mouth-watering chocolate to choose from!

❧ Virtual Presents
www.virtualpresents.com

Virtual Presents is a fun website for sending free virtual presents as postcards to friends and loved ones on the Net. You can choose from extravagant luxury items such as a brand-new Porsche, dream vacation photos, a romantic bouquet of flowers for your sweetheart, even a briefcase full of money. A great place to dream the day away!

Miscellaneous Freebies

Following are some miscellaneous freebies, including catalogs, freebies for parents, and various samples for the home.

❀ **Carnation Instant Breakfast**

   www.carnationinstantbreakfast.com (click on "Special Offers")

Sign up for the Nestlé Carnation Instant Breakfast e-mail newsletter to receive tips, recipes, and other special offers. This offer is available to residents of the United States only.

❀ **Claritin**

   In the United States, call 800-CLARITIN

   www.claritin.com

Claritin Syrup relieves seasonal allergy symptoms in children age two and older. Visit the website for a free $3 rebate certificate and product information. The Claritin website also offers other rebates off and on throughout the year. Check back at a later time if an offer is not currently available. This offer is available to residents of the United States only.

❀ **Frederick's of Hollywood**

   In the United States or Canada, call 800-323-9525

   www.fredericks.com (click on "Catalog")

To receive a free catalog featuring lingerie, bras, panties, clothing, shoes, legware, and other accessories, fill out the online request form or call. This offer is available to residents of the United States and Canada.

❀ **Instead SoftCup**

   In the United States, call 877-367-9636

   www.softcup.com

Instead SoftCup is a feminine protection product. It is not a tampon or pad but rather a soft little cup that you wear internally. Call for a free sample. This offer is available to residents of the United States only.

❀ **Martha Stewart Living Omnimedia, Inc.**

   www.marthastewart.com

To receive a free Martha Stewart catalog featuring products for cooking, gardening, entertaining, crafting, traveling, kids, babies, and more, request one from the website (click on "Catalog Requests"). This offer is available to residents of the United States and Canada.

In the United States and Canada, call 800-999-6518 to request a free trial issue of the *Martha Stewart Living* magazine, with no risk or obligation to buy. Call for further details. This offer is available to residents of the United States and Canada.

❦ No Brainer Blinds and Shades

FREE Safety Offer
Three Brainer Tower
4660 Beechnut
Houston, TX 77096
www.nobrainerblinds.com/info/child.html

Write to No Brainer Blinds and Shades to receive free cleats or breakaway safety tassels. These cleats and tassels are designed to help prevent strangulation from window treatment cords. Include a self-addressed, stamped envelope with your request. Be sure to affix a minimum of 43¢ postage for residents of the United States, and two Canadian postage stamps if you reside in Canada. The company will send you either two breakaway tassels or two cleats at no further cost. Write the word "tassel" or "cleat" on the return envelope, *not on your envelope to them.* This offer is available to residents of the United States and Canada.

For more information on making today's window treatments safer for young children, visit the website.

❦ Pepcid Complete

www.pepcidcomplete.ca/en/trialoffer/index.asp

Complete a brief survey at the website to receive a free trial-size sample of Pepcid Complete Chewable Tablets for heartburn relief, together with a coupon for your next purchase. This offer is available to residents of Canada only.

� Petit Danone
www.petitdanone.ca (click on "Promotions")

This site offers free promotional items from time to time. Visit the website to see what promotions are currently running. These offers are available to residents of Canada only.

✧ pHisoderm
www.phisoderm.com

Visit the website to sign up online for cool offers and free samples from pHisoderm. This offer is available to residents of the United States and Canada.

✧ Puzzle Club
www.puzzleclub.org (click on "Order a FREE Book")

Get a free thirty-two-page children's storybook, *The Puzzle Club Easter Adventure*. This offer is available to residents of the United States and Canada.

✧ Slim-Fast Foods Company
In the United States, call 877-375-4632
www.slim-fast.com

Sign up online to register for your free personalized diet plan and receive access to Weight Charting Tools, notification of special promotions and coupon offers, a free newsletter subscription, and more. This offer is available to residents of the United States and Canada. Call to request free "Get Started" materials, including a free *Little Book of Weight Loss Success* and personalized meal plan. This offer is available to residents of the United States only.

✧ Something to Remember Me By
www.somethingtoremembermeby.org

Something to Remember Me By is a legacy project designed to encourage closer relationships between parents, grandparents, and children. Free online activity theme kits are available at different times of the year. These activity kits are filled with intergenerational activities, crafts, a listing of books and websites that grandparents and grandchildren can share, and much more. Some examples of the different activity theme kits are Grandparents Day, the holidays, Valentine's Day, and Mother's Day. To get a free online copy of the latest activity kit that you can view or print out, visit the website. This website also offers free Grandparent Awards that you can print out for your child to give to her grandparents, as well as free Best Mom Award certificates, printable note cards, and more.

StartSampling
www.startsampling.com

Sign up online to request a free sample of Downy Enhancer or other promotional items. This offer is available to residents of the United States only.

Susan G. Komen Breast Cancer Foundation
In the United States or Canada, call 800-462-9273
www.komen.org

The Susan G. Komen Breast Cancer Foundation offers a free breast self-exam instruction card that is waterproof and can be hung in your shower. This handy reminder card illustrates and describes the techniques of breast self-examination. Call the Breast Care Helpline at the above-listed toll-free number to request a free card. You can also call the Breast Care Helpline for information about breast exams and breast cancer. This offer is available to residents of the United States and Canada.

Tide Fabric Care Network
www.tide.com/specialoffers

This website offers free samples and contests from time to time throughout the year. If a free offer is not currently available, check back again at a later time.

❦ T-Stick Disposable Thermometers
www.t-stick.com/freesample.htm

The T-Stick is a single-use cardboard thermometer that is used to quickly check if meat, fish, or poultry is thoroughly cooked. To receive a free sample, send a self-addressed, stamped envelope to:

Free T-Stick Sample
Trans World Services, Inc.
72 Stone Place
Melrose, MA 02176

❦ Victoria's Secret
In the United States or Canada, call 800-HER-GIFT
www.victoriassecret.com (click on "Request a Catalogue")

To request a free catalog from Victoria's Secret, call or visit the website. This offer is available to residents of the United States and Canada.

❦ Walt Disney World
U.S. website: http://disneyworld.disney.go.com (click on "Order your FREE Vacation Planning Kit today")
Canadian website: www.disney.ca/vacations/disneyworld/vpv

Planning a trip to the Magic Kingdom? Visit the website to order a free Vacation Planning Kit (video or DVD) to help make the most of your Walt Disney World vacation. This offer is available to residents of the United States and Canada.

Ways to Stretch Your Dollar

I remember, back in my "BD" (before diapers) days, a girlfriend telling me how things had changed drastically from the birth of her first baby to the birth of her third baby.

With her first baby she told me that she went on a clean streak, sterilizing everything from bottles to nipples, rattles to teething rings. When her first baby dropped his pacifier on the floor, she would immediately sterilize it in boiling water for several minutes before handing it back to him. But with the birth of her second baby, she eased up quite a bit. This time when her baby dropped his pacifier on the floor, she would pick it up, run hot water over it, and then hand it back to him. By the time her third baby came along, she simply picked the pacifier up off the floor, put it into *her* mouth, and then handed it back to the reaching arms of her baby. I remember thinking, "Bad Mommy! Bad Mommy! I'll never be so careless with my baby."

True to my words, when my first daughter, Kayla, was born, I, too, sterilized anything and everything that would even come in contact with her. I always bought the most expensive laundry soap, packaged especially for babies, in the rare case that my daughter would develop an insidious rash from the regular family laundry soap. I prewashed all of her brand-new baby clothes immediately after taking them out of the packages. I always gave my daughter a bath every day, sometimes twice a day if she was really dirty, and I was always sure to change her outfits the minute they were messy.

But my quest to be a perfect mom didn't stop there. I must have read more than ten parenting books before my daughter was even born to be sure I was extra prepared in absolutely every situation. *What to Expect When You're Expecting* was my bible. I poured over and clipped out articles from parenting magazines and—don't laugh at me when I tell you this—even neatly arranged the articles in file folders according to various categories (e.g., baby food, sleep, nursing).

In my quest to be supermom, I bought every gizmo and gadget on the market (many of them are still collecting dust in my closet). I spent a fortune on the latest baby toys, only to find that my baby enjoyed playing more with my car keys, the remote, and my cordless phone, not to mention the boxes and wrapping that all those expensive baby toys came in. As far as clothing went, I always tried to make sure that my daughter was dressed from head to toe in a perfectly matched, spotless ensemble.

Now, with the birth of my twins, I, too, have eased up in many ways. I give my babies a bath every two or three days and a quick sponge bath on the days they don't get a bath if they are really dirty. (That alone saves me tons of time and energy!) On wash days I throw my babies' outfits in the laundry with the rest of the family's dirty clothes, using my regular family laundry detergent, and they still come out smelling sweet and clean. I graciously accept hand-me-downs from friends and relatives, as well as whatever help and support they so kindly have to offer. As far as clothing goes now, sometimes I'm lucky if my babies are even wearing any, especially in the summer when it's really hot outside. But babies love to be naked, I reason, and they sure are adorable running around the yard naked as a jaybird, happy as a lark!

In fact, I try to do whatever I can to make my life easier and am always looking for the simplest and most efficient way to do things.

As a mother of three, I definitely feel more confident and don't find myself worrying so much about all the little things. Does it really matter if my child isn't weaned from her bottle by the time she reaches her first birthday? Do my babies care if they're wearing hand-me-downs or the latest designer fashions?

There are still, of course, many areas where I draw the line, especially when it comes to safety issues. Our house is like Fort Knox. I wouldn't have it any other way. Every cupboard is locked, medicines are tucked away safely, baby gates guard the top and bottom of the staircases, and safety covers are plugged into all the outlets. These things are too important to be overlooked.

I also enforce policies that are important for my children's health and development, like insisting that they wash their hands after going to the bathroom, say "please" and "thank you" as much as possible, clean up their toys at the end of the day, and—please—stay out of the toilet bowl!

Also, my children love books, crafts, and music. I always try to take time out to read to them or do a craft project with them every day. I won't scrimp on these things, as they are what provide my children the most enjoyment and, to me, are essential to their development.

As each parent is different, you have to decide for yourself what matters the most to you and what doesn't, what your priorities are and what you can let slip occasionally, what would make your life a little easier, and what would give you more time with your children, more time for yourself—and more sleep!

As far as obsessing about keeping the house clean, forget it. There are going to be many times when it will be next to impossible to keep your house clean—and besides, do you really have to finish the dishes when your daughter has just created her first finger-painting masterpiece and wants you to help her proudly display it on the fridge?

Financially, you have to learn how to question your purchases ("How much could I save if I switched from one brand to another?") as well as to resist your urges and impulses ("This baby shampoo costs twice as much as the other one, but it smells so much better"). And most important, you have to learn to do what makes you feel comfortable, not what you feel is expected of you from others.

When Kayla was born, I made some very expensive mistakes. But experience is a good teacher, and I have learned a few little tricks and tips along the way that I would like to share with you to help you, too, save money and have more quality time to spend with your precious new little one.

Here are some mommy-tested-and-approved ideas from a been-there-done-that mom who, after making some expensive mistakes the first time around, went on to save hundreds, if not thousands, of dollars when the twins were born.

Diapers

Babies go through a ton of diapers. Some days it seems like they poop twice their body weight! In the first three years of your baby's life, diapers will probably be one of your biggest expenses, as your baby will need more than six thousand diaper changes during this period.

Stock Up

As you can never have enough diapers, it's a good idea to start buying diapers early. Here's a great way to stock up on diapers in advance: When you get into about the fourth or fifth month of your pregnancy, start buying one package of diapers every week or every other week when you do your regular grocery shopping. Skip the newborn-sized diapers—you will probably only need one or two packages of them anyway—and buy the larger-sized diaper packs.

When we found out that we were expecting twins, we started buying diapers right away, one pack a week from my third month of pregnancy on, and when the twins came, we definitely knew that we had made a smart choice. Not one of those diapers went to waste!

Buy in Bulk

Another way to save on diapers is to buy direct from the factory at warehouse prices. Give the factory or warehouse a call in advance and ask if the public can make bulk purchases directly from the warehouse at a discounted rate. (This applies to other baby items as well.)

Check your local flyers to see when diapers go on sale in your area and stock up. Warehouse stores like Cosco also offer a great deal on diapers when you buy them by the case. Shopping this way can really save you a bundle!

Cloth Diapers

Cloth diapers seem to be becoming popular again. New accessories, such as cotton diaper wraps, diaper covers, and even felted wool diaper covers, are now available for your added convenience as well. When you buy cloth diapers, not only will you be saving money, but also you won't be adding to the landfill problem.

Diaper Pails

Being the mother of twins, I always had a difficult time trying to keep the babies' nursery smelling sweet with all the diapers the twins would go through. Here's a simple and inexpensive trick that I learned from another mom on how to eliminate diaper pail odors. Save all of your plastic grocery bags and empty bread bags. Put the dirty diaper into one of these bags, tie the bag in a knot, and toss it into your diaper pail. This method works similar to a Diaper Genie by keeping the odors locked in, except that it's free!

Formula

Another big expense in your baby's first year of life, should you decide not to (or not be able to) breast-feed, will be formula. There are a couple of simple ways that you can cut the costs of formula, ways that will really add up in the long run.

One way to save money on infant formula is by purchasing a store-brand formula instead of a name-brand formula. There are many store-brand formulas available, depending on where you do your shopping, and many of them are made by Wyeth Nutrition, including Parent's Choice Infant Formula, a great formula that you can purchase exclusively at Wal-Mart. These store-brand infant formulas can be up to 40 percent cheaper than the national name brands, saving you as much as $500 (U.S.) on the cost of formula in your baby's first year alone!

Many parents have the misconception that the cheaper formulas will not meet the nutritional needs of their baby, and that the more expensive brands have more to offer; however, the truth is that the less-expensive formulas contain almost the same ingredients as the more costly formulas.

To ensure that you are getting the best quality formula for your baby, no matter what price you are paying, the Infant Formula Act requires all baby formula manufacturers to follow specific procedures and guidelines when they make their formula. The ingredients found in infant formula are strictly regulated. The only difference is the price consumers pay.

You can also save money on the cost of infant formula by choosing powder formula over the more expensive concentrated liquid formula. The preparation of powder formula may require a little extra effort, but it will really save you money in the long run.

Baby Food

When your baby first begins to eat solids, she will only need a small amount of baby food per feeding. In the first few weeks it will seem like a lot of that leftover baby food goes to waste as it has to be thrown out after a couple days of being left in the fridge.

To preserve the leftover baby food, pour the food into the individual compartments of an ice-cube tray. Cover with plastic wrap and freeze. Once it's frozen, pop it out, put the cubes in a resealable bag, and place the bag back into the freezer. Take one or two cubes out each night, depending on the amount that your baby will need for the next day, and put them in the fridge to thaw overnight.

These individual cubes are the perfect size portions for your baby when she first starts on solids. With this method, you'll no longer have to spend the extra money buying the more expensive smaller-sized baby food jars; you can buy the larger sizes without worrying that anything will go to waste.

Another great way to save money on baby food is to make your own. Homemade baby food can help you provide low-cost, nutritious food for your little one.

Making your own baby food is really simple. You can puree the baby food in a blender or food processor and pour it into the individual compartments of an ice-cube tray in the same manner as just discussed. Another great thing about making your own baby food is that you know exactly what is going into it—no added salt, sugar, or starch and no unnecessary spices.

So get to work on your purees for some nutritious meals that your baby will love!

(For some great recipes on making your own nutritious, homemade baby food, check out the online recipes from Chapter 2, "Baby Freebies on the Net.")

Breast-Feed and Save

Breast-feed, and give your baby the best for nothing! There are so many wonderful benefits to breast-feeding, both to you and your baby—financial benefits as well. Moms who breast-feed their babies can save more than $1,000 (U.S.) a year in formula alone! Breast milk is free—it doesn't cost a penny. Should you choose to breast-feed, there are other things that you will save money on as well, including baby clothing (because formula stains can ruin an outfit and they are difficult to remove) as well as the cost of baby bottles and nipples.

Breast-feeding is definitely the best choice for your baby for many reasons:

Benefits to Baby
1. No baby formula measures up to mother's milk. Breast milk provides perfect infant nutrition. It also provides added protection against illnesses and diseases.
2. Breast milk helps pass meconium. Colostrum, or early milk, is designed to help move this sticky tarlike substance through an infant's body.

3. Breast milk is fresh. It is also more digestible than formula, as human milk contains an enzyme that aids in digestion.

4. Studies have shown that formula feeding increases a baby girl's risk of developing breast cancer in later life. Women who were breast-fed as children had a 25 percent lower risk of developing breast cancer than women who were bottle-fed as infants.

5. Studies have shown that formula feeding is associated with a lower IQ. Those who were breast-fed as infants had both better intelligence and greater academic achievement than children who were infant-formula fed.

6. While breast-feeding, the baby benefits from close body contact with the mother.

And if all of that's not enough reason for you to breast-feed, think of the benefits to yourself as well.

Benefits to Mom

1. Your body returns to its prepregnancy size faster. Lactation burns nearly five hundred calories a day, which results in quicker weight loss.

2. There is less postpartum bleeding in women who breast-feed their infants.

3. According to the American Academy of Pediatrics, breast-feeding for thirty-four months or more during your lifetime lowers the risk of certain cancers and reduces the risk of premenopausal breast cancer by 35 percent.

4. Breast milk is free!

5. Breast milk is readily accessible and is always warmed and ready to go. No formula to make, no bottles to sterilize, and no mess to clean!

If you are getting frustrated and are having problems breast-feeding your infant, don't give up! Contact the La Leche League (see Chapter 8, "Parenting Support Groups") for current breast-feeding information and tips.

Maternity Wear

When I was expecting my first daughter, I remember complaining to a friend that I had to buy expensive maternity clothes that I was only going to wear for a few months, and possibly a second time if we decided to have more children. The next thing you know, my friend disappeared into her basement and reappeared with a huge box filled with maternity clothes.

"Where did you get all of these clothes?" I asked. She told me that each of her friends at work who had recently given birth had passed on their maternity clothes for her to wear when she was expecting. She never had to buy a single maternity wear item, except for bras and underwear. "And now they're all yours," she said with a grin, dropping this huge box in front of me.

I was really glad to accept this unexpected gift from my friend, especially at a time when the endless list of things that I needed to buy for my baby was growing and growing. When I was expecting, I wore a lot of the maternity clothing from that box. After my baby was born, I put all the clothes back into an even bigger box, added a few of my own purchases, and passed them all back to my friend, who then passed this now quite huge box to another one of her expecting friends.

Don't be shy to approach friends, coworkers, and relatives who have recently given birth and ask them if you can borrow their maternity clothes. Chances are they won't mind a bit and will be glad that their maternity clothing can get more wear. Then, after you have given birth to your baby, put your maternity clothing in a box, and pass it on to another expecting mom. I'm sure she will really appreciate it!

Baby Clothes

When I found out that I was expecting, one of the first things I did was head out to the nearest Baby Gap and buy up almost everything in the store. I bought mass quantities of onesies, sleepers, booties, hats, and bibs. Those adorable brand-new baby clothes are hard to resist— and so-ooo cute!

Next, I headed over to the nearest department store and stocked up on baby accessories, baby bedding, bottles, grooming kits—you name it. I spent an absolute fortune!

A few months later my best friend, Diane, threw me a baby shower, where I received a bounty of beautiful baby clothes and other precious baby gifts. Thanks to doting grandparents, my new baby's wardrobe was better than my own! I ended up with stacks of stuff for my baby, way more than I would ever possibly be able to use.

My advice is to wait until after your baby shower to start buying clothing for your baby to make sure you buy only the items you really need and to avoid duplication. Chances are you'll receive lots of beautiful baby outfits, sleepers, and other baby accessories at your baby shower, enough that you may not need to buy many new items yourself.

Another great idea is to register for your baby shower at Babies "R" Us, Toys "R" Us, Sears, or any other store that offers a free baby registry. When registering for a baby shower, you can list exactly what you need. Registering for your baby shower in advance also makes it easier for friends and relatives who are unsure of what to buy for the baby. (See "Drop-In Freebies" in Chapter 3, "Free Stuff from Stores," for a list of some companies that offer free baby registries.)

Get the word out that you will gratefully accept any and all hand-me-downs. Both of my sisters-in-law and my best friend gave me boxes and boxes of baby clothing. Most of the items were in excellent condition, some had never been worn, and the ones that had been worn were perfect to be used for outside play and for baby to wear around the house.

When I was pregnant with my twins, Shane and Katie, I was very lucky. I hardly bought any new outfits for my babies as I received tons of great hand-me-downs from friends and relatives. (It seems that when people find out you're expecting twins, clothing just pops up from everywhere!) Most of the clothing that I did buy myself for the twins came from secondhand stores.

Secondhand Treasures

When my first daughter was born, the sky was the limit! I spent a fortune dressing her from head to toe in designer baby outfits. By the time my twins came, I realized I could no longer afford this luxury.

I have to thank my sister-in-law, Kelly, for getting me hooked on "second-time-around" stores. I highly recommend these stores for baby wear. You can find a wealth of designer baby clothing at these stores, and for a fraction of the cost. Some of the clothes you find at these stores have hardly been worn and look brand-new. Many of these stores also carry slightly used baby furniture, as well as baby toys, accessories, swings, and more, usually in excellent condition.

If you are lucky enough to find one of these stores in your neighborhood, you are well on your way to saving money!

Keep in mind that you can also sell baby's outgrown clothes to many second-time-around or consignment stores. Use this money to buy new clothes or other items for your baby.

Garage Sales

Another great way to get terrific deals on baby clothing is at garage sales. In our neighborhood on a Saturday morning, you can't make a simple trip to the convenience store without passing a garage sale. They're everywhere!

You wouldn't believe some of the great deals I've gotten at garage sales in my neighborhood. People were practically giving away their baby clothes. I bought huge boxes filled with baby clothes for only five bucks!

Buy Off-Season

A great time to buy baby clothing is off-season. Many stores put their winter clothes on sale during the late winter or early spring, and their summer clothing on sale during the late summer or early fall. You can get great deals buying off-season, sometimes even saving more than 50 percent off the original price.

Designer Clothes

I can't say I blame you for wanting to splurge on some adorable designer outfits for special occasions, but try to keep these purchases to a minimum, maybe one or two. Your baby will look absolutely adorable in that little velvet, lacy designer dress, but the spit-up will look the same as it did on that secondhand sleeper—and besides, you'll find that your baby will be much more comfortable in a 100-percent-cotton sleeper than that itchy, scratchy, get-this-thing-off-of-me, lacy dress!

Coupons and Discounts: Clip 'n' Save

One of the simplest and most effective ways to save money on baby products is to browse through your local newspaper for money-saving coupons on baby items. Ask your friends and family to clip out any baby product coupons that they find in magazines and newspapers and save them for you. The ones you don't need you can always swap with friends, relatives, or other mothers at work.

Online Coupons and Discounts: Click 'n' Save

Another great way to collect valuable discount coupons is through the Internet. Following is a list of websites that offer a multitude of free printable grocery coupons, retail coupons, coupons for baby products, and more. You can download and print out your coupons.

To make your online search for coupons and discounts quicker and easier, many of the sites listed offer a convenient search option, allowing you to hunt for a particular item by typing in a search word, such as "diapers," after which you'll be taken directly to a list of the companies that offer discount coupons on diapers. Many of these websites list their offers in several different categories (e.g., baby products, baby clothes, toys, groceries, and food coupons) to help direct you to exactly what it is you're looking for. Some websites even have special features where you can search for discounts and coupons in your area only, by state, province, or city.

Keep in mind that you should never have to pay a fee to get coupons online. Be wary of websites that request that you pay a monthly or a one-time fee to receive their coupons and discounts.

If you don't have access to a computer, either borrow one from a friend or try to get online at your local library; many libraries now have Internet access available to the public at no charge. Happy hunting!

❀ BargainShopping.org
www.bargainshopping.org

A portal for penny-pinchers, this website offers links to over five hundred online stores currently running sales, coupon offers, and more.

❀ Bigcoupons.com
www.bigcoupons.com

Bigcoupons.com offers tons of free money-saving coupons—food coupons, retail coupons, and more—that you can print out. These offers are available to residents of the United States and Canada.

❀ BudgetMom.com
www.budgetmom.com

For the frugal mom, BudgetMom.com offers freebies and printable coupons to help families save money.

❀ CoolSavings
www.coolsavings.com

CoolSavings offers grocery coupons, store coupons, free samples, gift certificates, rebates, and more. Sign up and save! This offer is available to residents of the United States only.

❦ CouponSurfer.com
www.couponsurfer.com

At CouponSurfer.com, you can select coupons by clicking logos, browsing different categories, or doing a search. A wide assortment of online discount coupons is offered in several different categories, including baby and maternity coupons, books, clothing, food, grocery coupons, and more.

❦ DailyeDeals.com
www.dailyedeals.com (click on "Online Coupons")

At this website you can search for money-saving coupons from many different websites that offer baby products, such as the Disney Store, Gap, and OshKosh B'Gosh. You can find discounts on baby gifts, baby clothes, toys, children's books, and other baby stuff. Many of these websites have special clearance sales where you can receive a discount of more than 50 percent.

❦ Factory Outlets
www.outletbound.com

At this website you can receive a free "Shop Like a Pro" VIP voucher redeemable at more than 160 participating outlet centers nationwide. Save hundreds of dollars the next time you go shopping! This offer is available to residents of the United States and Canada.

❦ Frugal Shopper Canada
www.frugalshopper.ca

This website offers free coupons, contests, and other free stuff to Canadian shoppers.

❦ H.O.T.! Coupons!
www.hotcoupons.com

When you register at this website, you will get an e-mail to let you know what coupons are available in your area. You can also search this website by category as well as by typing in your ZIP code or geographic location to find coupons in your area. This offer is available to residents of the United States only.

✿ Valpak

www.valpak.com

This website offers free printable coupons for the whole family! Simply type in your ZIP code or postal code to see what is available in your area. This offer is available to residents of the United States and Canada.

✿ ValuPage

www.supermarkets.com

ValuPage is a collection of manufacturer-sponsored offers that are good on leading brands, distributed throughout the Internet. Honored in over fifteen thousand supermarkets in the United States, ValuPage offers a chance for busy families to receive discount coupons at their grocery store. Visit the website for further details. This offer is available to residents of the United States only.

Free Samples from Your Doctor

The next time you visit your doctor for a checkup, ask if any free samples are available to you and your family. Many doctors receive boxes of free promotional samples and other items from time to time and would be glad to share them with you. Don't be afraid to ask.

If you suspect that you are pregnant and haven't yet purchased a home pregnancy test for confirmation, check with your doctor or local health clinic first; most of them will provide a free pregnancy test.

Things You Should Never Buy Used

Don't scrimp on safety!

Crib

There are numerous requirements that must be met by the companies that manufacture infant cribs, and for good reason. Cribs are associated with more children's deaths than any other juvenile product. According to the Danny Foundation, more than ten thousand children are injured in unsafe cribs every year, seriously enough to require hospital treatment.

A crib is something that you should never buy secondhand. An old crib may contain lead paint, which, if ingested, can be extremely dangerous. In addition, some of the slats on older cribs are too far apart and could entrap your baby's head. According to the U.S. Consumer Product Safety Commission, crib slats should be no more than 2⅜ inches apart. The mattress in your baby's crib should be firm and fit snugly; it should not be too small for the crib, as your baby could accidentally slip in between the crib and the mattress. Make sure your crib meets the current national safety standards. (Visit the U.S. Consumer Product Safety Commission website, listed in Chapter 6, "Web Resources for Parents," for more information on product safety rules and regulations, as well as product recalls.)

Car Seat

The second thing that you should never buy used is an infant car seat. If a car seat has been in even a mild car crash, it may have been weakened and may not hold up in another crash. When you buy a used car seat, there is no way of knowing if it has been in a car crash. In addition, some of the older car seats may not meet today's safety standards. It's better to be safe than sorry.

Baby Swing

A baby swing is another thing that I do not suggest buying used or borrowing from a friend. According to the U.S. Consumer Product Safety Commission, approximately 1,200 children under age two suffer swing-related injuries annually.

There are several features that a swing should contain to keep it safe:

- A crotch restraint and a seat belt
- An adjustable seat that you can recline for a newborn and raise as his neck gets stronger
- Speed control so you can choose a gentler, slower swing motion for a newborn and a faster swing motion for an older child
- Easy in/out access
- Braces between the legs of the swing for extra support

Some other things to keep in mind:

- Follow the safety instructions that accompany your swing.
- Do not attach toys with a long string to the swing.
- Do not put a pacifier on a cord around a baby's neck.
- Supervise and keep your baby in view.
- Stop using the swing once your baby can grab the swing's legs.

All-Time Best and Worst
Baby Items

I'm astounded at some of the extravagant baby items I've seen on the market over the last couple of years, popping up at upscale baby stores all over Canada and the United States. The "upscale baby," whose parents shop at these trendy stores, can be seen about town wearing luxurious leather suits and animal print dresses, suede-fringed jackets, designer jeans, and faux-fur jackets. These little tykes are really stylin'! Their wardrobes are better than my own!

One of the latest fashion trends to hit the market is perfume for babies. Hello? Are they serious? One of the things that I loved most about my babies was their sweet, natural scent. (I often found myself sneaking into their room while they were sleeping just to smell them. I couldn't help myself. They smelled so-ooo delicious!) As far as I'm concerned, no perfume can match that sweet, heavenly scent.

However, for a new baby, especially a firstborn, many parents think the sky's the limit! When you are out shopping for your baby, the salespeople will make you think you need to buy everything. A new mom is an easy target, shopping at an emotional time and wanting to make sure that her baby has the best of everything.

The truth is, there are lots of things your baby can live without. You really don't need to have all the latest gizmos and gadgets on the market today.

The best thing you can do, before heading out to the department store, is make a list of the things that your baby *really* needs and stick to it. Stop buying things that *may* come in handy. You will probably never use them. When in doubt of what to buy, think about what baby items your mother used. I'm sure she didn't have near the amount of baby items that are on the market today, and she did just fine—didn't she?

My Top-Ten List of Totally Useless Baby Items

Think how much you could save by eliminating only a few, if not all, of the infant unnecessaries in the following list.

1. **Infant Shoes.** Those little infant shoes certainly look cute in baby pictures, but an infant doesn't really need shoes until he is learning to walk. Skip 'em!

2. **Baby Kimonos.** My husband calls them "The Hugh Hefner Designer Housecoat for Babies." Although they really do keep your baby all wrapped up and cozy-warm, a nice fluffy bath towel that is big enough to wrap your baby from head to toe is all you really need to keep your baby warm and dry after a bath.

3. **Baby Powder.** Baby powder is a definite no-no. Besides the fact that it is unnecessary, it's also very dangerous and harmful to your baby's lungs if inhaled. Cross it off your shopping list. To keep baby dry, make sure you towel-dry your baby well after a bath. Be sure to get into all of the little cracks and crevices under the arms and legs. A layer of petroleum jelly is all you need to protect your baby's bottom from moisture. Frequent diaper changes will help to prevent diaper rash. If your baby does develop a serious diaper rash, pediatricians recommend zinc oxide.

4. **Crib Bedding.** Pass up the $200 to $300 elaborate, showy crib bedding sets that include a comforter and a pillow. They look great in a nursery, but according to the American Academy of Pediatrics, "It is not

recommended for baby to sleep with a comforter, pillow, or other soft bedding. Babies should be put to sleep on their backs with a firm, flat mattress. This can help reduce SIDS (Sudden Infant Death Syndrome), as well as suffocation. All you really need to buy are a couple of fitted crib sheets."

5. **Changing Table.** Many new parents think their baby's nursery isn't complete without a changing table. I had one and only used it once. To me, changing tables are the biggest waste of money. They are quite expensive and can take up a lot of space in the nursery, not to mention that they are dangerous as well. As strange as it may sound, the safest place to change a diaper is on the floor or on a bed with a washable plastic changing pad placed under your baby's bottom. No matter how wiggly your baby gets, it is impossible for her to fall off the floor. Most infants can wiggle themselves right off a changing table in a split second, which may result in serious injury or even death. Why take the chance? Keep in mind, too, that sometime after your baby's first birthday, she will probably be too big to change on the changing table and you'll end up changing her on the floor or bed anyway. But if you do have your heart set on getting a changing table, get a changing table/dresser combination that can be used by your child for many years to come.

6. **Baby-Wipe Warmers.** For those of you who don't know what a baby-wipe warmer is, it's exactly like it sounds—a warmer that is supposed to heat baby wipes to an even temperature and make changing time more comfortable for baby. The warming unit attaches to a changing table, crib, or countertop. Parents have found that, yes, these warmers do heat up the baby wipes, but the problem is that these warmers heat from the bottom and have a tendency to "cook" the wipes, turning them brown and even burning the bottom ones. Don't waste your time, money, or wipes on this useless product.

7. **Brush and Comb Set.** They make nice keepsakes but aren't really necessary. The last time I looked, most babies don't have a lot of hair. But if your baby is born with massive amounts of beautiful hair, any clean comb or brush with soft bristles will do the trick.

8. **Baby Carriers.** You don't need a baby carrier separate from your car seat. Spend your money on a good combination car seat/carrier. The

best thing about these car seats is that when your baby falls asleep in the car, you simply remove the baby carrier from the car seat and carry baby inside the house, without having to wake him up by taking him out of his car seat.

9. **Cradle or Bassinet.** You really don't need a cradle or bassinet if your baby's crib will fit in your room. When our twins were born, they slept in their separate cribs in our room until they were big enough to be moved into their nursery. You use the cradle for a very short period of time anyway, as most babies only fit in them for a few months. My advice is to spend your money on a good solid, adjustable crib.

10. **Bathtub Seats.** Both useless and dangerous, infant bathtub seats are rings that are designed to keep your baby sitting upright in the bathtub. They can be quite dangerous as the suction cups on the seats can come unstuck, allowing the baby to easily tip over into the tub. Babies have drowned while using bathtub seats and rings. I had one but only used it once. It was uncomfortable and awkward for my baby, and besides, it was much more fun for me to take a bath together with my baby! If you do decide to use one of these seats, *never* leave your baby alone in the bathtub, not even for a second.

Knock these useless baby items off your shopping list and save your money for the things you will really need to buy, like diapers—*lots of diapers!*

I'd Love to Hear from You!

Send me an e-mail with your list of totally useless baby items, and I may post them on my website or even use them in my next book. (See the Introduction for my contact information.)

Things You Can't Do Without

Following is a list of some of the things you may want to have readily available when you arrive home with your new baby, as well as some of the items that will make your life easier in the first year of your baby's life.

1. **Diapers, Diapers, Diapers!** Let's face it—life without diapers would be . . . well . . . very messy!

2. **Onesies.** One-piece baby outfits, or onesies, are great because they won't slide up your baby's back. These combo T-shirts and bottoms won't pull up like regular T-shirts, plus they help to hold the baby's diaper in place. The best type of onesies has snaps at the baby's crotch, making diaper changing much easier. Buy the adjustable ones with different snap positions that will allow the outfit to grow with your baby. You'll definitely need lots of these, but wait until after your baby shower to buy them, as you will probably get many as gifts.

3. **Baby Bibs.** One item to stock up on when you're having a baby is baby bibs. You will need many of them for when your baby spits up, for when your baby starts on solids, and if you have a baby that drools a lot. My babies often kept their bibs on throughout most of the day. I found that it was much easier to simply put on a fresh new bib than to change their entire outfit every time they would spit up. It also saved money, as their outfits would stay newer and cleaner for a longer period of time. And fewer outfit changes = less laundry!

4. **Safety Items.** Safety items for your home are essential, something you definitely don't want to scrimp on. Children have a wonderful sense of curiosity, which, unfortunately, may get them into trouble. Be sure to take the time to go through your home carefully to find all the areas that might be unsafe for a little one. Get down on your hands and knees and inspect your home from top to bottom, using a baby's eye view. Some of the items you should consider purchasing to help baby-proof your home are outlet covers, cabinet latches, drawer locks and latches, baby gates, and toilet locks. (For a few simple ideas on making your own electric cord holders, baby choke testers, and more, see Chapter 13, "Why Buy It When You Can Make It!")

5. **Nursing Bra.** If you are planning on nursing your baby, you're going to need a good nursing bra. In my opinion, any nursing bra that

you can't unfasten with one hand in one second is useless. When your baby is fussy and crying because he's hungry, you don't want to be messing around with a bra that is difficult to unfasten. Spend a little extra money to buy a good nursing bra, and wait until your last month of pregnancy to be sure of the most accurate sizing. Playtex and Motherwear both have excellent, highly rated nursing bras that will meet all of your needs.

6. **Bouncy Seat.** Infant bouncy seats are priceless! They provide a safe place to put your baby and are really convenient, as they can be situated in any room of the house. They also come in handy when your baby first starts on solids. As your baby probably won't be able to sit upright in the high chair at this point, you can feed her right in the bouncy seat. We used the vibrating type of bouncy seat, which always helped to put our babies to sleep. The attached musical toy bar was an added bonus, as the lights and music kept our babies entertained.

7. **Jolly Jumper or ExerSaucer.** Another safe place to put your baby while you are busy, perhaps in the kitchen preparing meals, is a Jolly Jumper or an ExerSaucer. Once your baby is big enough, a Jolly Jumper that you can hang in the doorway, or an ExerSaucer that you can place in the kitchen or any other room of your house, can be a great place to put your baby, providing lots of fun and entertainment, as well as exercise, for your little one.

8. **Waterproof Changing Pad.** You'll definitely get lots of use out of these! To protect your crib mattress from accidental leaks while your baby is sleeping, place a waterproof changing pad under your baby's crib sheet directly on top of the crib mattress. You might also want to purchase an extra one to carry in your diaper bag to always have a clean place to change your baby when you are out in public. You can use them on the floor or on the bed—actually, you can use them anywhere—to change your baby! Many of these changing pads also come with a separate removable cotton or flannel cover that you can put over the pad. It can easily be removed and simply thrown into the laundry when it gets dirty.

9. **Breast-Feeding Cream.** If you're going to breast-feed, I highly recommend using breast cream. I used it when I nursed all three of my babies. It really helped with cracks and sore nipples. Lansinoh makes a great breast cream that is made with pure lanolin. It is perfectly safe for baby as well.

10. **Rompers.** Rompers look so adorable on the little ones! Rompers with feet are great to help keep your baby's feet warm at night and throughout the day—which comes in handy, since it's almost impossible to keep a pair of socks on a baby for any length of time.

I'd Love to Hear from You!

Send me an e-mail with your list of baby items that you can't do without, and I may post it on my website or even use it in my next book! (See the Introduction for my contact information.)

The Top Ten Hottest Baby Items in Hollywood

For today's celebrity moms, the urge to splurge is taken to new levels as the Louis Vuitton diaper bag ($1,120) and the Silver Cross Pram ($2,499), known as the Rolls Royce of baby carriages, are the latest must-haves in Hollywood. The sky's the limit as celebrity moms head to Posh Tots for such extravagant items as the Circus Sleigh Crib ($2,904) and the fairy-tale-inspired Goldilocks crib ($3,484) to transform their baby's nurseries into a dream world.

When it comes to maternity wear, the chicest Hollywood accessory to be seen with is a "bump." Today's hottest celebrity moms are proudly displaying their bumps and curves with the latest, ultra-hip maternity wear—cleavage and curves accentuated. Sarah Jessica Parker, always the fashionista, elevated pregnancy to a whole new level of hip by dressing her baby belly in the trendiest low-cut, super-short maternity fashions available.

Pregnancy is chic, fashion-conscious, and—most shocking of all—sexy. Women today want to celebrate their pregnancy, not hide it. Being pregnant has never been so fashionable! So get ready, girls, for a list of the hottest baby items and maternity wear on the market today.

1. **Fleurville MotherShip Pink Stripes Diaper Bag.** How would you like to carry the same diaper bag that was featured on the Oprah show? Courteney Cox has it, Sarah Jessica Parker has it, . . . and so can you! Featured in top fashion magazines as one of the best diaper bags around, it features a vibrant striped exterior, red interior lining, multiple interior pockets, and an insulated bottle sleeve. It can be yours for $149.95! www.diaperbags.com.

2. **Maternity Jeans.** The latest maternity jeans are ultra-hip, belly-baring low risers by 7 for All Mankind, Earl Jeans, Joe's, Bella Dahl, and Citizens of Humanity. Worn by celebrity moms Gwyneth Paltrow, Debra Messing, Liv Tyler, and Kate Hudson, these fashionable jeans are worn under the belly with adjustable waistlines. They look fabulous with a bump! Sarah Jessica Parker, who never missed a fashion beat when she was expecting, could be seen about town showing off her bulging belly in Seven maternity jeans, the ever-popular, low-slung jean made for two. www.apeainthepod.com; www.lizlange.com; www.naissancematernity .com; www.veroniquematernity.com.

3. **Silver Cross Kensington Pram Carriage.** The Kensington pram from Silver Cross was the baby carriage of choice for Brooke Shields, who loved the carriage so much that she had it flown in from Northern England for the arrival of her daughter's birth. Silver Cross prams are handmade in England, each with a numbered plaque, and have transported such luminaries as Princess Diana's and the Queen's children. www.silvercrossbaby.com.

4. **Patemm Diaper Changing Pads.** Courteney Cox is crazy about the Patemm diaper changing pads. Their bright colors and floral patterns are certain to catch the eye of baby Coco. An alternative to the rectangular changing pads, these pads are round so you can lay your baby down any which way. www.patemm.com.

5. **Wrap Dresses and Wrap Blouses.** Gone are the days of tentlike maternity dresses. Today's maternity dresses and blouses look like they came off the runway in Milan! The style-savvy moms of Tinseltown, including Liv Tyler, Catherine Zeta-Jones, Lisa B, and Jada Pinkett Smith, look absolutely fabulous in today's cleavage-baring attire by such designers as Diane von Furstenberg and Liz Lange. www.apeainthepod.com; www.naissancematernity.com; www.lizlange.com; www.veronique maternity.com; www.mommychic.com.

6. **Posh Tots.** To create the ultimate Hollywood nursery, Posh Tots (which furnished Ross's and Rachael's baby nursery on *Friends*) carries such extravagant nursery items as a $40,000 pumpkin-coach bed straight from Cinderella to offer your baby the royal treatment, as well as luxurious baby bedding, cashmere baby blankets, and more. Sarah Jessica Parker, Reese Witherspoon, and Princess Caroline have furnished their babies' nurseries with this extravagant collection. www .poshtots.com.

7. **Maternity T-Shirts.** A favorite with celebrities, maternity tanks and tees with cute slogans such as the popular "Lovin' My Buddha Belly," "Goddess with a Bump," and "Blossoming Baby Belly," have been seen on celebrity trendsetters such as Kate Hudson. There are also "daddy tees" for the father-to-be that bear the cool slogan, "Men Who Change Diapers Rule!" www.preggersnproud.com.

8. **Wetsuit Onesies.** For the hippest line of baby clothing, check out Generation Z Baby, the ultra-trendy store for surfer-cool baby outfits including tees, onesies, and baby wetsuit loungewear. A favorite line of Courteney Cox, Britney Spears, Liv Tyler, Julia Roberts, and Angie Harmon, these adorable outfits come with built-in kneepads. According to Daddytypes.com, "It's for women who wear yoga pants and Juicy Couture everywhere, who question why they have to get their kid dressed in the morning." www.generationzbaby.com.

9. **The Belly Balm.** Used to butter up the bodies of Bobbie Brown, Uma Thurman, Cindy Crawford, and Josie Bissett, this nourishing skin cream by Baby Basics helps prevent stretch marks. When actress Kelly

Preston was expecting, The Belly Balm was her most indispensable pregnancy product. "I rubbed it all over my stomach and thighs every night before bed," says Kelly of this remarkable skincare product. www.spacadet.com.

10. **Limited Edition Baby Outfitters Valco Stroller.** How do celebrities gear up for baby? With this stroller. According to Laurie Hibberd of CBS News, this is the hot new stroller that Julia Roberts used for her twins, Hazel and Phinnaeus. With reclining seats, padding, and back support, this attractive and fashionable stroller, as seen on *The Early Show*, comes in ice blue and ice pink and is sold exclusively through Baby Outfitters. www.baby-outfitters.com.

Why Buy It When You
Can Make It!

There are multitudes of ways you can save money on baby products, arts and crafts, toys, baby clothing and accessories, and safety items. Be resourceful. Take a look around your home for items that can double as baby toys. Use ingredients you can find in your own kitchen cupboard to make terrific arts and crafts for your little one. Be creative and use your imagination to make all sorts of cost-saving baby items!

Baby Products

Here are some great money-saving ideas to make your own brand of baby products, including baby wipes, diaper rash cream, child safety items, diapers, and more. They are simple to make and great to use in a pinch when your supplies start running low.

Emergency "Diaper"

All out of diapers and baby needs to be changed, now? Use a cotton T-shirt! Any size will do, but the bigger the shirt, the better the absorbency.

Place the T-shirt on a flat surface. Fold in the sides to form a tapered end (cross over each side in the middle) at the T-shirt hem. Place baby's bottom on the center of the T-shirt, and wrap the sleeves around baby's tummy. Bring tapered end up, fold over overlapped sleeves, and tuck in. Pin securely.

Emergency Diaper Cover

Need a diaper cover in a hurry, and they're all in the wash? Use a plastic bag!

For a baby weighing less than sixteen pounds, cut a "T" shape out of a grocery bag; use a garbage bag for a bigger baby. Cut the bottom part of your "T" about 10 inches (25 centimeters) wide on the bottom fold of the plastic bag. This will be the crotch part of your emergency diaper cover. Cut the top part of your "T" across the width of the plastic bag. This will form the waist ties. Make your "T" about 8 inches (20 centimeters) high for small, 10 inches (23 centimeters) high for medium, or 13 inches (33 centimeters) for large. Cut the sides of your "T" curved, for better coverage. Cut open the waist ties so you can tie them on over baby's diaper. Ties can be about 20 inches (51 centimeters) long for small, 23 inches (58 centimeters) for medium, or 27 inches (69 centimeters) for large. (Trust me, it sounds more complicated than it is.)

When you open up the cover, you should have a giant "H" shape. Place a folded prefold diaper inside, place baby on top, and tie at each side of baby's waist.

If you really like this style of diaper cover, you can cut some more out of waterproof, ripstop nylon for no-sew, indestructible, washable tie-on diaper covers.

Diaper Rash Remedy

(Thanks to Jennifer for this frugal baby tip.) To prevent diaper rash and chafing, use aloe vera, either the fresh plant or the extract bought at the pharmacy or health food store. It saves money and is a great barrier cream. It also works great on teething rash around the mouth, as it is not harmful to swallow.

Baby Wipes (1)

Here's a great idea that all moms should know about—how to make your own homemade baby wipes!

Cut a large paper towel roll in half to form two cylinders each about the size of a roll of toilet paper. (Use high-quality, thick paper towels.) Next, mix together 2 cups warm water, 2 tablespoons baby oil, and 2 tablespoons baby bath soap or baby shampoo. Put one of the paper towel half-rolls into an empty container with a lid or an empty baby wipes container. (Use only one of the half-rolls per batch.) Pour the liquid mixture directly on top of the paper towel roll and cover. After the liquid has completely saturated the entire roll, remove the cardboard tube. Pull your wipes from the middle of the roll. Keep sealed. Voilà!

Baby Wipes (2)

(Thanks to J. Buffett for this frugal baby tip.) Use facial tissues for your baby's bottom, rather than the homemade baby wipes. Fill a squirt bottle with 2 to 3 tablespoons baby wash, 2 to 3 tablespoons baby oil, and 2 cups water. Squirt his bottom, then wipe with the dry tissues.

Baby Laundry Bag

(Thanks to Beth for this frugal baby tip.) Use an old pillowcase for a laundry bag in the baby's room. Attach it to the changing table by a diaper pin. It keeps all of baby's dirty things together, and when it's time to wash, everything can be dumped right into the washing machine, including the pillowcase!

Toilet Roll Protector

Save that toilet paper! To prevent your toddler from unrolling the entire roll of toilet paper and stuffing it into the toilet, make your own toilet roll protector by recycling a plastic 2-liter pop bottle. Cut the bottle top and bottom off to form a toilet roll cover about 4¾ inches (12 centimeters) wide. Cut a slot in this cover, to pull the toilet paper through, about

½ inch (1 centimeter) high and 3 inches (7½ centimeters) across. Remove your toilet roll and spindle from the wall mount, slide both inside your new toilet roll protector, and reattach to the wall mount. This should at least slow your toddler down!

Economical Baby Bassinet

(Thanks to Candace for this frugal baby tip.) For families who cannot afford a bassinet, wicker laundry baskets make great substitutes.

"With my oldest son, I used a wicker laundry basket as a bassinet, and I kept it beside my bed at all times. I could take it to the living room or anywhere else I needed as well. With my other two children, I used a plastic laundry basket and lined it with several layers of blankets to use as a place to keep them by my side during the day."

Stuffed Toy Net

Here's an idea to make your own toy net to match your baby's nursery decor and hold all of baby's stuffed toys.

Just cut out a triangle of strong, stretchy fabric measuring about 40 inches by 40 inches by 60 inches (or 1 meter by 1 meter by 1½ meters). Tie each corner of this triangle tightly to a metal ring and suspend the net in a corner of your baby's room with hooks screwed into the wall. Fill with toys!

Nursery Bookends

(Thanks to Renata for this frugal baby tip.) Make bookends out of stuffed animals. Undo the back of the stuffed animal. Take out some stuffing and fill with marbles. Resew by hand. To prevent sliding, glue some rubber matting on the bottom of the toy. This works great for matching the decor in your baby's room!

Hair Detangler

Does your child have tangles from baby-fine hair? Rather than buying those expensive bottles of spray-on detanglers, try making your own frugal alternative. Mix one part conditioner with ten parts water. (You may need to experiment. Some conditioners work better for this than others.) Pour into an empty, cleaned-out spray bottle. Spray this frugal detangler solution on your child's hair, and comb those tangles out easily.

Nonslip Cup

Wrap one or two wide rubber bands onto your child's cup. The rubber bands will give your child a better grip, and the cup won't slip out of her hands as easily.

Baby Choke Tester

Every home should have a choke tester to check if toys and other objects are safe for baby play. Commercial choke testers can be very difficult to find, very expensive, and too small to be effective.

Did you know that you already have a frugal baby choke tester right in your own home? (No, I don't mean the baby. . . .) An empty toilet paper tube!

Commercial choke testers are made to the government regulation size of $1\frac{3}{8}$ inches in diameter. However, the U.S. Consumer Product Safety Commission has reported many deaths of babies and children who have choked on objects slightly larger in diameter than this.

Your ordinary toilet paper tube is $1\frac{5}{8}$ inches in diameter. You can consider any toy or object in your home that fits inside this tube to be a choking hazard to your baby or child.

Cord Holders

Extra-long electrical wires, including extension cords and phone cords, may trip your little one—and are tempting for your baby to tug or chew on. Cord holders will hold those loose wires snugly against the wall.

Just cut two or more pieces of sticky-back Velcro 1 inch (5 centimeters) wide and about 2 inches (10 centimeters) long. Place the Velcro pieces with the sticky-back side along your baseboard, or wall, wherever the cord runs along, 1 to 2 feet (30 to 60 centimeters) apart. Stretch your cord out tight, and place the other side of the Velcro over the top of each piece attached to the wall, to hold the cord in place. Use as many pieces of Velcro as you need to hold the cord securely to your wall.

Childproof Bottle Tops

When your childproof bottles are empty, save the bottle tops. Wash them out and store in your kitchen drawer. When you buy something in a bottle that you wouldn't want your child to get into, but it doesn't come with its own childproof top, just check your childproof bottle-top stash for a bottle top that fits! Some pharmacies will also give you a childproof bottle top free, upon request.

Baby Clothing and Accessories

For those of you who are good at sewing, put your sewing skills to use and save money by sewing your own baby clothing, baby bibs, curtains, and accessories for the nursery—even nursing and maternity wear. Fabric stores carry a great selection of patterns for adorable baby outfits and nursing wear. Choose a simple pattern and use it again and again, using an assortment of different fabrics.

Following are a few simple ideas to make your own baby clothing and accessories.

Baby Mittens

(Thanks to Arlene for this frugal baby tip.) Forget about those tiny mittens for winter babies. Use older brother's or sister's woolly socks—clean, of course! They pull up high enough that baby can't get them off easily, and snow can't get in either.

Instant "Bib"

All you'll need are two "suspender" clips and about 10 inches (25 centimeters) of fabric elastic to be able to make a bib for your baby, instantly, wherever you are. Just fold each end of the elastic around the loop of one of the suspender clips and stitch. Now you can use this handy gadget to clip a washcloth (or two, for heavy droolers!) or hand towel around baby's neck. You can also store it in your diaper bag for use on the go, using it with napkins at restaurants and other places.

Easy Baby Rompers

Make your baby a really cute-looking romper from an older child's T-shirt or tank top. Just make sure the hem of the shirt hangs a few inches lower than the baby's diaper crotch.

Stitch 2 to 3 inches (5 to 7½ centimeters) of Velcro loop (or two or three snap "heads") on the inside of the hem, center front, and 2 to 3 inches of Velcro hook (or two or three snap "holes") on the outside of the hem, center back. If you find the neck opening a bit too big, just overlap the fabric at the back of the neck, and add a dot of Velcro or one snap to hold it closed. Then you just slip your new baby romper on your baby and fasten at the crotch. How adorable!

Free Nursing Pads

Take an old cotton T-shirt and cut it up into 6-inch (15¼-centimeter) circles. Place three to six circles on top of each other, and sew two rows of stitching near the outer edge, about ⅛ inch apart, to prevent the edges from unraveling. These make very comfortable nursing pads that won't slide around much inside your bra.

Less Slippery Socks

(Thanks to Lisa for this frugal baby tip.) "As my baby is just starting to learn how to walk and it is cold in the evenings (the reason for not being barefoot), instead of buying socks with grips on the soles already, we buy the socks in the bulk bag and use puffy paint on the soles. If applied properly, it doesn't peel off (if you're worried about this, you can get the nontoxic kind). You can write anything you want on the soles of the socks, or draw pictures, and baby will have a better grip on the floor."

Arts and Crafts

When your baby is well past the stage of putting things into his mouth, here are some mommy-tested-and-approved arts and crafts recipes that you can make for absolutely fabulous fun!

I have used these recipes over and over again with my own kids. They are simple to make, and most of the ingredients can be found in your own kitchen cupboard! Many of these arts and crafts projects are as good as or better than store-bought products, but for a fraction of the cost. In fact, some of the projects in this section cost only pennies to make!

So roll up your sleeves and dress for a mess, because you're probably going to get really messy with these activities. And remember, a lot of the fun is in the preparation!

Clay for Baby's Handprints or Footprints

Here's a great idea to make an adorable keepsake for your baby. When this clay hardens, it dries to a nice matte finish and is great for all sorts of craft projects.

Here's What You Will Need

1 cup baking soda
½ cup cornstarch
1 tablespoon salt
¾ cup water
Large plastic margarine container

In a medium-sized saucepan, mix the baking soda, cornstarch, salt, and water. Heat on high until the mixture begins to boil. Turn heat to low and continue mixing until the mixture becomes thick and creamy and is difficult to stir. Remove from heat. Knead with your hands when cool. Next, place the clay into a large plastic margarine container and flatten out on the top. Have your baby place her hand or foot firmly into the clay to make an imprint. Use a toothpick or pencil to write your baby's name and birth date into the clay. Decorate with stones, shells, marbles, or small mosaic pieces. Let harden for a few days. (Be sure the clay is completely hardened before removing from the container or it may crumble.) If you would like to hang the ornament, use a straw to poke a hole into the top portion of the clay before it has hardened. Tie with a ribbon.

:Q: **Another Creative Idea.** Roll the clay with a rolling pin. Use Christmas cookie cutters to cut shapes into the clay. Use a toothpick or pencil to write your baby's name and date of birth in the clay. Poke a hole in the top of the ornament with a straw and hang on your Christmas tree with a ribbon for a cute, homemade baby's first Christmas ornament!

Jiggle Soap

When I created the recipe for this fun concoction, I had in mind two of the things that my children love the most: bath time and Jell-O! Put the two of them together and here's what I came up with. It's so-ooo cool! This amazing soap wiggles and jiggles and looks just like real Jell-O— but you can't eat it! Kids can play with it in the bathtub, wiggle it, jiggle it, squish it through their fingers, or even wash themselves with it. Bath time will never be the same again!

Here's What You Will Need

1 package gelatin (clear, unflavored)
½ cup hot water
¼ cup liquid bubble bath
Food coloring (optional)

In a small bowl, dissolve the gelatin into the hot water. Next, mix in the bubble bath and stir thoroughly. If you would like colored Jiggle Soap, simply mix in a few drops of food coloring. Refrigerate for at least four hours. Cut into cubes. Store in the refrigerator until ready to use.

:Q: **Other Creative Ideas.** Cut the Jiggle Soap into cubes and place in a plastic dessert bowl. The kids can squirt some of daddy's shaving cream or some kids' bath foam on top of the soap for a delicious-looking—but inedible—dessert. Great for bath time fun!

Make Fish-in-a-Bag by adding blue food coloring to the soap mixture to make "water," then pour the mixture into a plastic reseal-able bag. Add a plastic fish or another plastic sea creature to the bag to make Fish-in-a-Bag. Prop the bag upright in your fridge and refrigerate for at least five hours. Store in the refrigerator until ready to use. (You will need to triple the recipe to have enough soap to make this project.)

Pour the Jiggle Soap into jars or containers and tie with a ribbon to make a really cool party favor for a child's birthday party. (Store in the refrigerator until ready to use.)

Squishy Bag

When my twins were babies, they loved playing with the Squishy Bag. They would poke it, squish it, and throw it. It's a lot of fun for little ones and costs only pennies to make!

Here's What You Will Need

Glitter, metallic confetti, plastic fish, or other small toys
Large resealable bag
Water or hair gel
Strong tape

Throw some glitter, metallic confetti, or small plastic toys into a large resealable bag. Fill the bag up with water or hair gel and seal it closed with some strong packing tape. Let your little one play with the bag by poking and squishing it.

Note: You may want to have your child play with the bag outside, just in case it pops open.

:Q: **Parental Warning.** If you have placed small items in the bag that may be considered a choking hazard, please supervise your child at all times during play.

Play Dough

Here's a simple play dough recipe that you can make for your child using ingredients that you can find in your own kitchen cupboard. Make sure that children don't try to put the play dough into their mouth: this play dough tastes awful, but when has that ever stopped a curious little one!

Here's What You Will Need

2 cups flour
¾ cup salt
4 tablespoons vegetable oil
¾ cup water
Large mixing bowl
Food coloring (optional)

Mix the flour, salt, vegetable oil, and water in a large mixing bowl. Mix well and knead with your hands until smooth. If you would like to add color to your play dough, add several drops of food coloring to the water before you add it to the dry ingredients. Store in an airtight container in the refrigerator.

Homemade Bubbles

Children of all ages love bubbles. They are fun to blow, chase around, catch, and pop. The following three bubble recipes are much cheaper than store-bought bubbles, and they work just as well.

Here's What You Will Need

½ cup liquid dish soap
2 cups water
3 teaspoons sugar
Plastic bottles with lids

Mix together the liquid dish soap, water, and sugar. Pour the mixture into the bottles.

Note: Use nonbreakable plastic bottles for storing the bubbles. You don't want to use glass bottles that might shatter if dropped.

☼ **Other Creative Ideas.** You can make your own bubble wand by tying a pipe cleaner into a small circle, twisting it in the middle, and leaving the remainder of the pipe cleaner straight for the child to hold on to. For a unique bubble wand, try using a plastic strawberry container or the plastic holder from a six-pack of soda.

Monster Bubbles (1)

Mix up this simple concoction to make huge, monster-sized bubbles, then follow the directions to make a giant bubble-maker.

Here's What You Will Need

1 cup water
½ cup liquid dish soap
⅓ cup glycerin
½ teaspoon sugar
Plastic bottles with lids

To make huge, monster-sized bubbles, mix the water, liquid dish soap, glycerin, and sugar together, stirring well. Place the liquid in nonbreakable plastic bottles. Chill the mixture before use to make the bubbles last even longer.

To create a giant bubble-maker, bend a wire coat hanger into a circle with a short handle and wrap pipe cleaners or cotton twine around the loop. This enables the wand to hold more solution.

Monster Bubbles (2)

When your kids get bored, try mixing up a batch of this super-duper bubble solution to make huge monster-sized bubbles! (See earlier directions to make a giant bubble-maker.)

Here's What You Will Need

3 cups water
1 cup liquid dish soap

¼ cup corn syrup
Plastic bottles with lids

Mix together the water, liquid dish soap, and corn syrup. Stir well.
Place in nonbreakable plastic bottles.

Bubble Play
- Let your child blow bubbles through the wand. For the really
  little ones who tend to put the bubbles into their mouths, have
  them wave their arm through the air to create bubbles.
- Blow the bubbles for them and have them try to catch them in
  the air, clap them with their hands, and step on them.
- Give your child the bubble wand and have her try to catch the
  bubbles in the wand before they hit the ground.
- Try blowing the bubbles indoors. Turn on a child-safe fan and let
  the bubbles blow around the room as your child tries to catch
  them.
- Be adventurous. Let your child blow bubbles in the bathtub.

Giggle Goo

Young children love to get dirty, which is one of the reasons they really
enjoy this activity. This goopy substance is a favorite among children, as
they can't quite figure out how it works. They can pick it up like a solid,
and it will quickly "melt" through their fingers. At times it seems wet,
then dry. This goo will have your little ones giggling for hours!

Here's What You Will Need

Resealable bag, bowl, or baking sheet
1 cup cornstarch
½ cup water
Food coloring (optional)

You can make this mixture in a bowl or directly in a resealable bag.
First, measure the cornstarch and put it into the bag, holding it upright.
Then add the water and a few drops of food coloring, again holding the

bag upright. You can use your fingers or a spoon for mixing. Let your little one dig in with her hands and squish the goo through her fingers.

You may prefer to put the goo onto a baking sheet or in a plastic container and let your child play with it in that manner, as opposed to using a resealable bag where the goo may spill out. This mixture can be stored in the refrigerator for about a week. To reuse, just add some water and stir. Don't pour the goo down the drain, as it will clog.

Icebergs

These mini icebergs will keep your little one as cool as a cucumber on a hot summer's day. A great way to splash the day away!

Here's What You Will Need

Large plastic margarine containers
Water
Food coloring (optional)
Plastic toys (optional)

To make your icebergs, simply fill large plastic margarine containers with water and place in the freezer overnight. To remove the ice, run the containers under warm water. Set your icebergs afloat in a children's pool in the summer, or build a small snow fort or igloo in the winter. (To make huge icebergs, fill up large buckets with water and place outside in the winter to freeze.) You can add food coloring to the water before you freeze it for colored icebergs. Put a small plastic toy in the water before you freeze it. Your child will be pleasantly surprised when the ice melts!

☀ **Parental Warning.** Parents should always supervise young children who are involved in any water play activity.

Wet 'n' Wild Water Play

Little ones love the water. They just can't seem to get enough of it. Here's a terrific way to get a small child slowly used to water play. You'll turn a timid turtle into a frolicking fish in no time at all! Ready . . . set . . . get wet!

Here's What You Will Need

Large garbage bags, old plastic shower curtain, or plastic tablecloth
Hose or sprinkler

Spread some large garbage bags, an old plastic shower curtain, or a plastic tablecloth outside on the lawn. (You may want to tape the garbage bags together with some strong tape.) Turn on a hose or sprinkler, spraying some water directly onto the plastic surface. Sit your child, in his bathing suit, in the middle of the plastic sheet, where he can splash around in the small puddles of water.

☼ **Parental Warning.** Parents should always supervise young children who are involved in any water play activity.

Water Painting

Here are some simple ideas for water play that your child can try outdoors. You'd be surprised how busy these activities will keep her!

- Give your child a jumbo-sized paintbrush and a bucket of water. Have her paint the side of the house, the patio, the car, or whatever she wishes, with water. On a hot sunny day, she will enjoy watching as the water disappears in the hot sun.
- Fill a bucket up with some warm soapy water, give your child some sponges and towels, and let him help you wash your car.
- Let your child wash her tricycle, doll clothes, or other toys using a bucket of warm soapy water.

Miniature Snowman

With this fun wintertime activity, your child will have his own miniature version of Frosty the Snowman to play with whenever he likes!

Here's What You Will Need

Clean snow
Bucket
Large garbage bags
Plastic wrap or plastic bags

Have your child help you collect a bucket of clean snow from the backyard. Spread out several garbage bags on the floor, and place the bucket of snow in the middle of the floor. Let your child put on her mittens and make her own miniature snowman. She can even decorate her snowman if she wishes. When she's done, wrap the snowman in some plastic wrap or plastic bags and place in the freezer. It will keep for several weeks.

Snow Play

When it's too cold to play outside, why not bring the fun indoors?

Here's What You Will Need

Large garbage bags or towels
Large bucket
Clean snow
Spoons, pots and pans, cooking utensils, measuring cups, cookie cutters, sand pails and shovels, spray bottles

Spread several large garbage bags or towels in the middle of the kitchen floor. Collect a large bucket of clean snow from outside, and place it on the garbage bags or towels on the floor. Give your child several of the items listed above. Let him put on his mittens and dig tunnels in the snow and scoop the snow. He can use the cookie cutters to make "cookies" out of the snow, simply by pressing the snow into the cookie cutters and removing the snow shapes out onto a plate. (If you like, you can even freeze the "cookies" in the freezer.) Fill up a plastic squeeze or spray bottle with some water and food coloring and let your child "paint" the snow.

Alligator Soup

While you're busy cooking dinner in the kitchen, your little one can cook right along with you, making her own homemade "soup"! (Of course, this soup is only for alligators, so no tasting!)

Here's What You Will Need

Mixing bowl
Water
Large wooden or plastic spoons
An assortment of spices, rice, or a collection of outdoor goodies, including sticks, stones, leaves, acorns, and pinecones

Fill a large plastic mixing bowl with water. Give your child some wooden or plastic spoons to mix with. Have him create his own "soup" by adding spices, such as salt, pepper, garlic powder, and cinnamon, to the water. He can have fun stirring and mixing the ingredients together, making his own soup. Give him any leftovers that you are cooking with at the time, such as celery, carrots, corn, or rice, to add to his mixture. Take him on a nature walk in the morning and have him collect an assortment of "ingredients" for his soup, such as leaves, grass, acorns, pebbles, or whatever nature has to offer.

Candy Necklace

Here's a craft that is fun to make—and even more fun to eat!

Here's What You Will Need

Licorice whips or string
O-shaped candies, cereal, pretzels, or minidoughnuts (anything with a hole in it)

Cut licorice whips or string to the length that you would like your child's necklace to be. Knot at one end. Have your child string several O-shaped candies or O-shaped cereal, such as Fruit Loops or Cheerios, onto the string. Tie securely for your child to wear as a deliciously edible necklace.

Bathtub Goo

Okay. It sounds disgusting, and, yes, it definitely looks disgusting. But what does it feel like? Well, let's not go there. But children really do love it—honest! Your child can cover herself from head to toe in this gooey, slimy stuff—and the more she uses, the cleaner she'll get!

Here's What You Will Need

1 package gelatin (clear, unflavored)
1½ cups hot water
Food coloring
⅓ cup bubble bath
Plastic wrap
Plastic spiders and rubber worms (optional)

In a small bowl, mix the gelatin with the hot water. Stir briskly with a fork until dissolved. Next, add several drops of food coloring in the desired shade. Stir in the bubble bath. For extra-frightful bath time fun, mix in some plastic creepy crawlies, such as plastic spiders or rubber worms. Pour the mixture into a container and cover with plastic wrap. Refrigerate for about two hours. When it reaches a slimy, gooey consistency, it's ready for the tub. Let your child dig in and squish the goo between his fingers. Yuck!

Note: If the mixture has been left in the fridge for too long, it may harden. Simply set it out on the kitchen counter for about an hour until it turns slimy again. You can store the mixture in the fridge for a day or two until you are ready to use it, but keep in mind that you will have to let it sit out to soften it up again and to return it to its slimy consistency. This mixture washes off with water. Be sure to tell your child not to get it in his eyes, as it may sting.

Pop-Up Soap

Your little one will want to wash herself as clean as she can with this cute soap, just to get to the pop-up toy inside!

Here's What You Will Need

Clear natural glycerin soap (available at craft stores)
Glass measuring cup or microwave-safe bowl
Food coloring (optional)
Soap mold or plastic margarine container
Small toys, including small plastic dolls, figurines, rubber ducks, fish, dolphins, and other bathtub toys (do not use heat-sensitive items)
Plastic wrap

Cut soap into 1-inch (2 ½-centimeter) cubes. Place in a microwave-safe bowl or glass measuring cup and heat on high for about twenty seconds in the microwave. If soap is not completely melted at this time, continue heating at ten- to fifteen-second intervals until completely melted. (You can also melt the soap by placing it into a glass measuring cup that has been set in a pot of simmering water for about five minutes.) For colored soap, mix in a few drops of food coloring. Fill a soap mold or plastic margarine container with about 2 inches (5 centimeters) of the melted soap. Let cool for a few minutes, and then place the bottom portion of a small toy or another object directly in the center of the melted soap, leaving the top portion of the toy to remain outside of the soap, as if it were popping out of it. Place in the refrigerator to cool. When hardened, gently pop the soap out of the mold. Wrap soap in plastic wrap until ready to use.

☀ **Parental Warning.** Be very careful when melting soap. It can be extremely hot!

Picture Soap

Your child will love taking a bath with her own personal bar of soap, with a picture of herself or a special friend attached!

Here's What You Will Need

Bar of soap with a smooth, flat surface
Photograph or picture
Paraffin wax
Paintbrush

Cut a favorite photo to size, making sure it fits on the smooth surface of the bar of soap. You can also use colorful pictures from magazines or greeting cards or choose a cute cartoon character that your child loves. Using a paintbrush, brush some melted paraffin wax directly onto the flat surface of the soap and on the underside of the photo. Quickly place the picture firmly onto the flat surface of the soap. Next, brush a layer of melted paraffin wax directly over the top of the photo, brushing in one direction only, and covering the entire surface of the picture with the melted wax. When this has completely hardened, you may want to rub some vegetable oil onto the top surface of the picture with a paper towel to smooth the surface.

-☿- **Other Creative Ideas.** Wrap the bars in decorative paper and tie with a pretty ribbon, some raffia, or a bow.

As a special gift for your child to give to a friend, let her choose a favorite photo of herself and her friend together to attach to the bar of soap.

Soap Pump Surprise

One of the things that makes life interesting for the kids around our home are all of the little surprises I keep leaving around the house for them to find: small candy treats hidden in their shoes or tucked away in their coat pockets, bread and cheese slices cut into cute little star shapes, and a smiley face or cute little drawing on a steamy bathroom window. Here's an idea to make a little surprise that you can leave around the house for your child—and a great way to get your little one to wash his hands more often, too.

Here's What You Will Need

Clear plastic soap-pump dispenser (clear hand-soap or shampoo dispensers with clear soap inside work the best)
Assorted metallic confetti, shiny beads, buttons, small fabric flowers

Remove the pump from the soap dispenser, and add a small handful of metallic confetti, small beads, bright buttons, or other items that are small enough to fit into the opening of the bottle. Simply shake the bottle a couple of times to see it sparkle. Your child will actually enjoy washing her hands!

Ocean in a Bottle

Your little one will be fascinated by the swirling "ocean waves" when he rolls his Ocean in a Bottle along the floor, rocks it slowly back and forth, or shakes it up to see the magic!

Here's What You Will Need

Clear 2-liter plastic pop bottle with a screw-on lid
2 cups cooking oil
Funnel
Blue food coloring
Glitter, metallic confetti, and sequins
Water

Clean the plastic bottle thoroughly and remove the label. Pour the oil into the plastic bottle, using a funnel. Next, add several drops of blue food coloring and a handful of glitter, metallic confetti, and shiny sequins. Fill to the top with water. Replace the cap, and shake well. Be sure to screw the cap on tightly to avoid any leaks. (You might want to glue the lid on securely with a hot glue gun or some strong glue.) Have your child rock the bottle gently back and forth to make waves, shake it, or roll it along the floor.

Shimmering Bubble Bath

To add some extra sparkle to your child's favorite bubble bath or body wash, simply add some fine, loose glitter to the bubble liquid. She'll be sure to come out "sparkling" clean!

Easy Baby Toys

Don't spend a fortune on expensive baby toys for your baby. Babies don't care how much you spend on toys; in fact, some of the things they will love to play with the most can be found right in your own home! Here are some easy baby toys that you can make from recyclables and other common household items.

Beach and Sandbox Toys

Here are some great ways to recycle your quart- and gallon-size (1-liter and 4-liter) plastic bottles. First, clean the bottles out well.

- Cut a gallon-size bottle all around, about 6 inches (15 centimeters) from the bottom. Poke two holes on opposite sides near the top, attach a rope handle, and you have your sand pail. The remaining piece becomes your funnel.
- Cut another gallon-size bottle about 2 inches (5 centimeters) high and poke the bottom full of holes for a sieve.
- Cut the bottom off your quart-size bottle. Then cut a long U-shaped scoop, sloping your cut up along the sides. (If your bottle comes with a handle, make sure the handle ends up on the topside of the scoop.) This becomes your shovel.

The best part of these toys is that if they get left behind at the beach, you can always make more!

Instant Kite

Take one plastic grocery bag with handles, tie a long length of string to one handle, and *run!*

Free Toy Building Blocks

(Thanks to Linda for this frugal baby tip.) "I have one recycling tip for turning half-gallon square milk containers into toy blocks. Cut off the pouring end of two rinsed, dried-out milk cartons. Then push the two open ends together, pushing one carton inside the other. This doubles the strength of your new block and closes the ends.

"These are very lightweight and safe. I started this project while pregnant with my first child, and eight years later we have quite a collection—and it's always a favorite with visiting friends. They make great walls, forts, and cages for kids, as well as cities and roads for small cars."

Wooden Blocks

My children's grandparents made terrific wooden blocks for our kids out of untreated wood they bought at a hardware store. To make these simple wooden blocks for your kids, simply cut the wood into different-sized blocks and sand until smooth. You can also paint these blocks if you wish.

Indoor Sandbox

You can keep your little ones busy on a rainy "stay-in" day by creating an indoor sandbox. All you need is a large plastic dishpan and a 5-pound (2-kilogram) bag of cornmeal or rice for "sand," as well as some spoons, measuring cups, funnels, strainers, and so on. The cornmeal or rice vacuums up quickly and doesn't scratch the floor.

Baby's Discovery Board

Place a bulletin board or sheet of cork on the wall near (but out of reach of) your baby's bed or changing table. When objects and colors begin to fascinate your newborn, you can attach different objects and pictures to the Discovery Board for your baby to look at. Later, this can be a place to display your toddler's artwork. Watch out for the pins, though!

Things to Save Throughout the Year

Following is a list of things that you can collect and save throughout the year to make some terrific free toys, games, and other fun and creative play items for your baby—a great way to recycle!

Drums
- Empty coffee cans
- Pots and pans
- Wooden spoons

Shakers
- Empty margarine container, plastic bottle, or empty film container filled with dried rice or uncooked pasta

Tambourine
- Aluminum pie plate

Wrist Bells
- Several small gold or silver jingle bells strung together on an elastic band to make jingle bell bracelets, which can be tied around a child's wrist

Water Toys
- Turkey baster
- Measuring cups and funnels for pouring
- Squirt and spray bottles

- Sieve
- Styrofoam meat trays for boats

Educational Toys
- Cups for stacking
- Socks for matching
- Buttons for sorting
- Junk mail and old Christmas and birthday cards for sorting and opening

Games
- Plastic soda bottles for bowling pins
- Plastic lids and paper plates for Frisbees

Pretend Play
- Large cardboard appliance box for a play fort
- Smaller cardboard boxes to make cars, buses, and trains
- Paper bags and socks for puppets
- Old jewelry, shoes, scarves, hats, dresses, and so on for dress-up play
- White jacket, bandages, and popsicle sticks for a doctor's kit

The "Mess" Factor

Arts and crafts time with your little one can get very messy. That's just part of the fun! Here are some great ideas to help reduce the "mess" factor.

Art Smock

Make a full-body smock to cover your child's clothing by cutting a hole in the top of a garbage bag for his head and two holes at each side of the garbage bag for his arms. An oversized T-shirt can also be used to protect your child's clothing.

Great Floor Savers

Cut and open up garbage bags at the seams, and place them under your child's worktable or high chair to protect your floors from accidental spills.

You can also use old towels, drop cloths, or sheets of plastic to place under your child's work area. An old shower curtain or plastic tablecloth also works well to protect the floors from spills.

Shaving Cream Clean-Up

For a fun way to get your child's hands clean after finger painting or other messy art projects, give your child a squirt of daddy's shaving cream and have him rub it into his hands and arms to play with it to get clean. This is a fun way for your child to get clean and makes mommy and daddy's job much easier as well!

From the Author

We are anticipating possible future editions of this book. Have you discovered any new free items for new or expecting parents that are not listed in our book that are currently valid? Does your company have free offers that you would like to make available to new or expecting parents? Companies, government agencies, and support groups are invited to submit items for consideration in our next revised edition. A description and actual sample of your offer is best for us to review it and write up an accurate description. Please contact the author by e-mail with your submission. (See the Introduction for contact information.)

When submitting your offer, keep in mind that we want to keep our offers free. Your offer must be free, with no obligation to buy anything. It must be available to residents of the United States, Canada, or both, and it must be related to parenting, babies, or child care.